D1528060

REFLECTIONS ON THE PROBLEM OF RELEVANCE

REFLECTIONS ON THE PROBLEM OF RELEVANCE

By ALFRED SCHUTZ

**Edited, annotated, and with an
Introduction by Richard M. Zaner**

New Haven and London, Yale University Press, 1970

Copyright © 1970 by Yale University.
All rights reserved. This book may not be
reproduced, in whole or in part, in any form
(except by reviewers for the public press),
without written permission from the publishers.
Library of Congress catalog card number: 78–99840
Standard Book Number: 300–01221–7
Designed by Sally Sullivan,
set in Linotype Times Roman type,
and printed in the United States of America by
The Carl Purington Rollins Printing-Office
of the Yale University Press.
Distributed in Great Britain, Europe, Asia, and
Africa by Yale University Press Ltd., London; in
Canada by McGill-Queen's University Press, Montreal; and
in Latin America by Centro Interamericano de Libros
Académicos, Mexico City.

Contents

The work of Alfred Schutz has become increasingly well known since the publication of his *Collected Papers,* the first volume of which appeared in 1962.[1] The second edition of the only book-length study published in his lifetime—*Der sinnhafte Aufbau der sozialen Welt,* first published in 1932—appeared in 1960,[2] and in a quite excellent English translation in 1967.[3] With the latter, Schutz's stature as a major philosopher and social

1. *Collected Papers* (The Hague, Martinus Nijhoff), *1, The Problem of Social Reality,* edited, with an Introduction by Maurice Natanson, 1962; *2, Studies in Social Theory,* edited, with an Introduction by Arvid Brodersen, 1964; *3, Studies in Phenomenological Philosophy,* edited by Ilse Schutz, with an Introduction by Aron Gurwitsch, 1966. (Hereafter referred to as *CP 1, CP 2,* and *CP 3,* respectively.)
Some scholars who have explicitly acknowledged the influence of Schutz are his long-time friend and colleague Aron Gurwitsch, whose major work, *Théorie du champ de la conscience* (Paris, Desclée de Brouwer, 1957) *(Field of Consciousness* [Pittsburgh, Duquesne University Press, 1964]), is dedicated to Schutz and includes a brief treatment of his theory of relevance; Maurice Natanson—see, for instance, the collection of his essays, *Literature, Philosophy and the Social Sciences* (The Hague, Martinus Nijhoff, 1962), and his forthcoming *The Journeying Self: A Study in Philosophy and Social Role* (Reading, Mass., Addison-Wesley Pub. Co., 1969); Peter Berger, *Invitation to Sociology* (New York, Doubleday Anchor Books, 1963), and in the volume coauthored by Thomas Luckmann (the editor of Schutz's final unfinished book, *Die Strukturen der Lebenswelt), The Social Construction of Reality* (New York, Doubleday Anchor Books, 1966); Harold Garfinkel, *Studies in Ethnomethodology* (Englewood Cliffs, N.J., Prentice-Hall, Inc., 1967); and Gibson Winter, *Elements of a Social Ethic* (New York, The Macmillan Co., 1966).
2. Published by Julius Springer (Vienna, 1932; 2d ed. 1960).
3. *The Phenomenology of the Social World* (Evanston, Northwestern University Press, 1967), tr. George Walsh and Frederick Lehnert, with an Introduction by George Walsh.

theorist began to be widely recognized. Since the publication of these works, a volume of essays edited by Maurice Natanson in memory of Schutz is in its final stages of preparation.[4]

During the last decade of his life, Schutz was actively engaged in writing another major study but was unable to complete it before his untimely death in 1959. Through the active and devoted efforts of his wife, Ilse Schutz, this final work—*Die Strukturen der Lebenswelt*—will soon appear in a German edition brought into book form by Thomas Luckmann and will then be translated into English by myself and Tristram Engelhardt.

Among others of Schutz's papers and lectures was discovered the present manuscript. The original version was handwritten in English between August 1947 and August 1951, mainly during his infrequent vacations in Colorado. It was conceived as Part I of a five-part study and was to be entitled, *The World as Taken-For-Granted: Toward a Phenomenology of the Natural Attitude*. Part I bore the title, "Preliminary Notes on the Problem of Relevance." After careful deliberation and detailed consultation with Mrs. Schutz, and with the advice of Professor Luckmann, it was decided that although Schutz had not planned to publish this portion of the study as it stood, I should undertake to bring it into publishable form. This task proved to be of major proportions and thus calls for a brief word of explanation.

The original text was in handwritten form; a typescript was also at hand, however. Both of these were made available to me by Mrs. Schutz. Inasmuch as Schutz's English version was in extremely rough form, an initial and crucial question had to be faced: whether to rewrite it completely, using the original as my guide; or whether to tamper as little as possible with it and, retaining its original "preliminary" flavor and style, merely to bring it into linguistically acceptable shape. For several reasons which I believe to be conclusive, and with Mrs. Schutz's agreement, I opted for the latter.

4. Maurice Natanson, ed., *Phenomenology and Social Reality: Essays in Memory of Alfred Schutz* (The Hague, Martinus Nijhoff, 1969).

In the first place, even though the study was conceived as only the first of five parts, I believe it can and does stand alone as a separate piece, important in its own right. And while some of the issues with which it is concerned are treated elsewhere in his writings,[5] Schutz's analysis of them here is much more detailed and, in any event, of sufficient strength and inherent value to merit separate publication. Finally, the growing interest in Schutz's thought, among students as well as established scholars, seems to warrant its publication as an important research document. The excitement of watching a really seminal mind "at work" struggling with one of the fundamental issues of the theory of social reality—even though he does not fully succeed in analyzing it here—provides by itself a sound reason. Unfinished and sketchy as it is in some respects,[6] those of us who continue to work at these issues will find significant insights and fruitful directions for our own thinking here.

The original text did nevertheless require considerable rewriting, in view of its very rough form. I have, however, attempted throughout to retain its original style and character and have added nothing to it. In order to make it more intelligible, I did find it necessary to provide extensive notes. Hopefully, these will succeed in filling out the study and in providing interested scholars and students with sufficient explanations of its central concepts and with numerous references for their further study of Schutz's other works and of the issues themselves.

A final word on the text is necessary. Although Schutz did have a table of contents for this study, I have revised it somewhat for the purpose of achieving further clarity in his analysis and its development. Thus his "Introductory Remarks" were originally planned to fill five long sections (perhaps even

5. Notably in one posthumously published essay, "Some Structures of the Lifeworld," *CP 3*, 116–32; to some extent in "Multiple Realities," *CP 1*, 207–59; and one lengthy section in *Die Strukturen der Lebenswelt*.

6. One section, on a theme of the Greek skeptic Carneades (included as Chapter 2 here), was regarded by Schutz as ready for publication as it then stood; other sections, however, are in mere outline form. These are all indicated in the footnotes.

chapter length), but he noted that they "have to be entirely rewritten." Apparently only an outline, it consisted of twelve handwritten pages; still, the subsequent sections (or chapters) were numbered consecutively from VI through X. My revision consists solely in placing the "Introductory Remarks" as Chapter 1 and renumbering the subsequent ones accordingly— with one exception. What appear here as Chapters 4 and 5 were originally one chapter. In view of its length and because there seemed to be a natural division in it, I decided to make it into two chapters. All other textual modifications are of a more or less minor nature and are mentioned in the footnotes.

The central features of Alfred Schutz's thought—its indebtedness to other thinkers, as well as its originality—have been treated at length in a number of other places.[1] In addition, of course, his own articles and book are readily available in several languages. It does not therefore seem appropriate or advantageous to rehearse them here. I shall rather try to place the present study in the context of his total work and then to suggest what strikes me as its major significance.

Schutz conceived his central thematic concern variously as a "philosophy investigating the presuppositions" of daily life, a "piece of phenomenological psychology," a "phenomenology of the social world," "the constitutive phenomenology of the natural attitude," and in his last major work, as an inquiry into the "structures of the lifeworld." In a more informal way, in lectures given at The Graduate Faculty of Political and Social Science of The New School for Social Research, where he lectured for many years in sociology and philosophy, he was fond of characterizing his concern as seeking to determine "what makes the social world tick."

Two major theses are at the heart of Schutz's work: (1) our commonsense knowledge of the world of everyday life (the

1. See, for instance, the various introductions to the *Collected Papers* and *The Phenomenology of the Social World,* and the other works cited above in n. 1 of the Preface. Also, see R. M. Zaner, "Theory of Intersubjectivity: Alfred Schutz," *Social Research, 28,* No. 1 (Spring 1961), 71–93; and Aron Gurwitsch, "The Common-Sense World as Social Reality—A Discourse on Alfred Schutz," *Social Research, 29,* No. 1 (Spring 1962), 50–72.

"lifeworld" or "the natural attitude") is a system of constructs of its typicality; and (2) this lifeworld is conceived as the constituted texture of interlocking activities of actors on the social scene, that is, it is a world *shared* with a multiplicity of other individuals living and acting within it in common, in mutually interlocking activities.[2] The system of typicality constructs is largely taken for granted without question (although they may be and sometimes are brought into question to one degree or another). But while we in our daily lives do periodically bring into question one or another taken for granted segment or construct of our lifeworld, the fundamental theses constitutive of the social world itself—its "taken-for-grantedness" and its "commonness"—remain unthematized by us in the context of our daily lives. In fact, Schutz contends, man in his natural attitude makes constant and unquestioned use of a specific *epoché*. He suspends all doubt of the world, its objects, and other living beings; he refrains from the doubt that they might not be, or might be otherwise than they are assumed without question to be (or otherwise than they appear to him to be).

Accordingly, in order for us to raise these as issues, to make them thematic for our analysis, it is necessary to make this "epoché of the natural attitude," as Schutz calls it, itself thematic; it is essential to refrain from refraining, or to practice an epoché on the "epoché of doubt." Only by focusing our attention on these constitutive theses of the lifeworld is it at all possible to accomplish the "phenomenology of the lifeworld," or, synonymously, the philosophical elucidation of the presuppositions or foundations of social reality. This second epoché means, then, the effort *to make explicit* precisely what is implicit and taken for granted by the very nature of commonsense life—to make its foundational presuppositions explicit for the sake of disclosing its structures, analyzing its strata, revealing its interconnected textures; and thereby to make it possible to understand what makes the social world tick, that is, what makes the social world at once "social" and "world."

2. Thus one of the fundamental themes in his work is the problem (or, as he preferred to say, the problems) of intersubjectivity.

It should be obvious as well that Schutz's effort to execute this project is at the same time a critical inquiry into the foundations of the empirical sciences which purport to deal with man and his sociocultural world. All such sciences begin at the outset with this lifeworld as already given and amenable to their various techniques and methods, and thus necessarily begin as well by presupposing the kind of foundational inquiry to which Schutz devoted himself. Conversely, although the phenomenologist of the lifeworld has much to learn from these empirical social, behavioral, and humanistic sciences, he cannot avail himself of either their methods or their theories. His inquiry is systematically autonomous. But precisely because it is presupposed by these sciences, it will have profound epistemological and methodological implications for them. Which "methods" and "concepts" the latter can legitimately use, after all, is strictly dependent upon *what it is* (the "subject matter") to which these methods and concepts purport to be applicable. The foundational analysis and explication of the "social," "behavior," and the "human" is necessarily fundamental to the determination of which methods and concepts are appropriate and justifiable. Hence, the "phenomenology of the social world" is at the same time the "phenomenology of the social (behavioral, humanistic) sciences."[3]

The present study of relevance brings to partial fruition an insight which Schutz had, in his first studies, only dimly seen. The social (or life-) world, he contended, is not simply one homogeneous affair. To the contrary, taking his clues from Edmund Husserl, William James, and Henri Bergson and extending their ideas in a highly original way, he argued forcefully that the social world is articulated into "multiple realities." It is

3. For further elaboration of this theory of the grounding of the social sciences, see Schutz's *The Phenomenology of the Social World,* esp Ch. 5; also the essays in *CP 1,* esp. "Common-Sense and Scientific Interpretation of Human Action," 3–47; "Concept and Theory Formation in the Social Sciences," 48–66; "Phenomenology and the Social Sciences," 118–39; and "Husserl's Importance for the Social Sciences," 140–49.

toward the elucidation of this central notion that the study of relevance is primarily directed, for it turns out to be, I believe, the principle at the root of the stratification of the lifeworld.

Analyzing our sense of reality in the well-known chapter of his *Principles of Psychology*,[4] William James holds that reality means simply relation to our emotional and actional lives. Whatever excites and captures our *interest* is real; hence to call something real is to say that it stands in some relation of interest to ourselves. The whole distinction, he argues, between what is real and what is unreal is grounded on two mental facts: "first, that we are liable to think differently of the same; and second that, when we have done so, we can choose which way of thinking to adhere to and which to disregard."[5] Our primitive impulse or tendency is to affirm straightaway the reality of whatever is experienced or conceived, so long at least as it remains uncontradicted. Or, as Jean Piaget would assert, so long as there is no obstacle encountered, the fundamental tendency of all human activity is to assimilate the universe to itself.[6] Since, however, we can and do "think differently of the same," and thus can choose which way to adhere to now and which at another time, two further factors emerge. First, there are numerous (probably an infinite number of) orders of reality, each having its own particular style of existence—which James calls "sub-universes," mentioning such examples as the worlds of sense or physical things, of scientific theory, of ideal relations, of religion, of madness, and so on.[7] Second, although we commonly conceive these subuniverses more or less disconnectedly and even tend to forget or obscure the others and their interrelations while dealing with one, everything we experience or think about is ultimately referred to one of these subworlds. "Each world," James asserts, "whilst it is attended

4. William James, *Principles of Psychology* (2 vol. New York, Henry Holt Co., 1890), 2, Ch. 21, 283–322.

5. Ibid., p. 290.

6. Jean Piaget, *The Origins of Intelligence in Children* (New York, International Universities Press, 1952), Ch. 1.

7. James, pp. 291 ff.

to is real after its own fashion; only the reality lapses with the attention."[8] As Schutz continually emphasizes, both Husserl and Bergson had had this signal insight, but it is especially Husserl whom Schutz found most relevantly and deeply concerned with exploring the foundations of this phenomenon. Still, Schutz's work, in the best Husserlian tradition, gives a highly original and more extensive treatment to it.

What James had touched on, consciously restricting himself to its psychological aspects, Schutz believes to be "one of the most important philosophical questions."[9] To appreciate this, however, it is necessary to free it from its psychologistic setting. Accomplishing this, he finds himself faced with two central tasks: on the one hand, to delineate more exactly these subworlds (or what Husserl had called "unities of sense" or "meaning") which constitute the lifeworld, to determine their interrelations and which among them can be called "paramount;" on the other hand, he must make explicit the essential ways in and by which these "sense-unities" are constituted, how they arise and are maintained within the lifeworld in typically taken for granted fashion, and which principle or principles govern the mind's choice in giving the "accent reality" to one or another of them at any particular moment. The first task Schutz accomplishes generally in his analyses of the world of everyday life, and it has been that facet of his work that has received the most attention. The second task is largely the burden of the present preliminary study (and, as already noted, forms an important part of his last work); it is, thus, less well known even though it is decidedly fundamental to what is to be accomplished under the first task. To appreciate the central place and importance of the phenomenon of relevance, as well as the specific sense Schutz gives to it, requires a brief review of several of his basic conceptions of the structures of the lifeworld.

James had spoken of a "sense of reality" which can be in-

8. Ibid., p. 293.
9. Schutz, "Multiple Realities," *CP 1*, 207.

vestigated in terms of a psychology of belief and disbelief.
To free this insight from this restriction, Schutz writes,

> we prefer to speak instead of many subuniverses of reality
> of *finite provinces of meaning* upon each of which we may
> bestow the accent of reality. We speak of provinces of
> *meaning* and not of sub-universes because it is the meaning
> of our experiences and not the ontological structure of the
> objects which constitutes reality.[10] Hence we call a certain
> set of our experiences a finite province of meaning if all of
> them show a specific cognitive style and are—*with respect
> to this style*—not only consistent in themselves but also
> compatible with one another.[11]

He goes on to describe the essential features of each such
finite province of meaning, noting that any of them may "receive the accent of reality," or be attended to as real. But within
our lifeworld, he stresses, there is no formula for passing from
one to another of these provinces (for instance, from the world
of dreams to that of waking life, or from that of scientific
theory—working in a laboratory, for instance—to that of
fantasy, as in a movie). The transition from one to the other is
always experienced as more or less of a "shock" (a "leap" in
Kierkegaard's sense, he holds)—precisely because each province has its own specific style (of concerns, language, objects,
actions, and so on).[12]

Although these remarks do pertain to the lifeworld generally,
there is a decisive qualification that must be made, for one of
them "is the archetype of our experience of reality. All the
other provinces of meaning may be considered as its modifica-

10. Schutz here refers to Husserl, *Ideen zu einer reinen Phänomenologie und phänomenologischen Philosophie,* Band I (Halle, Max Niemeyer, 1913) (later included in *Husserliana,* Band III [The Hague,
Martinus Nijhoff, 1950], Eng. trans. by W. R. Boyce Gibson [New York,
Macmillan, 1931]), Sec. 55: "In a certain sense and with proper care
in the use of words we may say that *all real unities are 'unities of meaning'.*" (Husserl's italics)

11. Schutz, "Multiple Realities," p. 230.

12. Schutz gives many examples of these, ibid., pp. 231–59.

tions."[13] This is what Schutz calls "the world of working," and is thus our "paramount reality." It is the world of physical things, including my own body; it is the realm of my locomotions and bodily operations, and thus offers resistances which require my efforts to overcome them; it places tasks before me and is the setting in which I carry out my plans and tasks, and in which I fail or succeed. "Working" means "gearing" into the outer world, which indicates that I as an actor on the social scene know that my bodily actions in and on the world change it, modify the objects in it and their various relations (and that I in turn am changed and modified by them)— changes that are experienced by me and my fellowmen such that they are able to "see" what I have done and I what they have done. I know my actions have causal efficacy as well as being productive of values and ends which I seek to realize. It is the world shared with others, not only individuals with whom I am acquainted and others whom I know less well or not at all, or groups of others also known more or less well or not at all, but also a world peopled with the "products" of others (cultural tools and artifacts, institutions, values, recipes for acting, and the like), all of which intrinsically refer to others. But gearing into the world of working also includes communication, hence it is the world in which language has its primary locus and origins; in it I meet, act and interact with, listen and respond to, others of all sorts—friends, strangers, enemies, children, relatives, students, colleagues, and so on.

This world in which each of us lives, works, and has his being, is taken for granted as "our reality"; so far as I must come to terms with it and take my bearings within it (with and among my fellowmen), I must understand it, and to this extent it is given to me as such for my experience and interpretation. I take it for granted that this world existed before my birth and will continue to exist after I die (hence, my lifeworld reveals several dimensions of "others" in addition to my contemporaries—viz. my predecessors and successors), and that it was and will continue to be a sociocultural world organized, experi-

13. Ibid., p. 233.

enced, and interpreted by my predecessors and successors in ways that are typically similar to those in which I myself and my fellowmen now organize and interpret it. Insofar as it refers to the world handed down to me (by my "tradition"), this assumption combines with the knowledge derived from my own experience to form what Schutz calls my "stock of knowledge at hand." By means of this progressively sedimented stock of experiences, the objects, events, and fellow beings I encounter and deal with in the course of my life are experienced by me as "things of such and such a kind," in other words as "types" ("strangers," "friends," "foreigners," "postmen," "politicians," as well as "trees," "dogs," and the like).

The world of working is at once the framework and the object of my actions. To carry out my plans and projects, I must act on it, change it, and experience its resistance to my efforts; thus, in my paramount reality my interest is pre-eminently pragmatic.[14] Moreover, this reality is oriented and structured for each of our actions in a spatiotemporal continuum, with my actual "Here" and "Now" functioning as a kind of center O of a system of actional coordinates determining the organization of my surrounding field of action. As such, my world is organized into a hierarchy of "zones" within my actual, potential, and restorable "reach," at the locus of which is my immediately available "manipulatory sphere"— each of these zones having its own particular typical spatiotemporal horizons and structures. These zones of interlocking actual, potential, and restorable sets of experiences are taken for granted by each of us as the unquestioned but always questionable matrix for gearing into the world.

At any moment, then, I find myself in a biographically determined situation which, although only in a small way due to my own experience, I must define and come to terms with in order

14. Ortega y Gasset's analysis of "the social" in his *Man and People* (New York, W. W. Norton, 1957), bears striking parallels to Schutz's study. Cf. esp. Ch. 3–5, and Ortega's notion of "pragmata." Though there are important differences between these two thinkers, there are numerous important convergences, a study of which would be quite rewarding.

to make my way in the lifeworld. Not to act in a particular situation is as constitutive of my biographical situation and stock of knowledge as if I were actually to gear into the world actionally. Hence, too, my situation is essentially *historical:* it is the sedimentation of all my previous experiences, and this "stock of knowledge at hand" is that in terms of which I act at any moment, that through which I interpret and experience the lifeworld.

Thus, within the taken for granted context of daily life, this "world" is not a mere object for thought nor primarily for knowledge, but a field of action and domination.[15] But we are not equally interested in all the strata of the world of working at every moment, nor in all the other provinces of meaning simultaneously. Therefore, what Schutz (in his paper, "Multiple Realities") calls "the selective function of our interest" organizes and structures the world into spheres of "major or minor relevance." How I define situations, which features of what objects I at any moment and place attend to or select as "interesting," as "calling for attention," or as "needful," depends upon "what I am doing" (my "plan of action" or "project at hand") prevailing at that time and place—and, as Schutz stresses, ultimately upon my "plan of life" generally. But this "what I am doing," this or that project at hand, does not itself simply fall from nowhere, full-blown and ready to go. Moreover, my ultimate plan of life is not itself just given to me all at once, nor created by me out of nothing. Each of my projects at hand is itself determined by something—and it is to this something that Schutz addresses himself with his conception of "relevances." The concept of "interest," as he argues in the present study, is not only too ambiguous to articulate the principle involved here, it is also not entirely accurate inasmuch as it is too psychologistic. What is at stake, indeed, is *a principle*

15. Schutz is in fundamental agreement with Bergson that (to use Bergson's case in point) perception is not initially in the service of information but rather of action. Cf. Bergson, *Matière et mémoire* (Paris, Presses Universitaires de France, 1939), esp. Ch. *1 (Matter and Memory,* [London, Allen and Unwin, 1911]).

of structurization of the lifeworld itself, a principle that is also determinative for my various interests and plans within the lifeworld in the sense that it is what accounts for "why" I turn to "this" rather than to "that" at "this" time in my life, in the course of "this" action. As he expressed it in "Multiple Realities,"

> I am, for instance, with the natural attitude, passionately interested in the results of my action and especially in the question whether my anticipations will stand the practical test. As we have seen before, all anticipations and plans refer to my previous experiences now at hand, which enable me to weigh my chances. But that is only half the story. *What* I am anticipating is one thing, the other, *why* I anticipate certain occurrences at all. What may happen under certain circumstances is one thing, why I am interested in these happenings and why I should passionately await the outcome of my prophecies. It is only the first part of these dichotomies which is answered by reference to the stock of experiences at hand as the sediment of previous experiences. It is the second part of these dichotomies which refers to the systems of relevances by which man within his natural attitude in daily life is guided.[16]

In this essay, written in 1945 and apparently the first time he clearly saw the crucial significance of relevance, Schutz confessed that he could not in this place unravel all the implications of the phenomenon. What he had recognized, nevertheless, was a point of immense importance: our every action, thought, and deed in the lifeworld (as in every finite province of meaning) is guided by and founded on a "whole system of relevances." Not only do such relevances determine the "selective function of our interest," which is itself a fundamental feature of our paramount reality, but they also determine, as Schutz tries to show in the present study, what Natanson characterizes as the "traffic between worlds."[17] The "accent of

16. Pp. 227–28.
17. Natanson, Introduction, *CP 1,* xliii.

reality" is bestowed on one or another finite province of meaning as a function of one particular project at hand, and this
in turn is determined by specific types of relevances. Hence,
the careful analysis of these systems of relevance became an
urgent task for Schutz's lifelong effort to comprehend the full
reach and texture of the lifeworld. The significance of the
present study, then, lies not in its being a thoroughly worked
out theory of relevance (which it is not), but in its posing the
fundamental questions clearly and precisely—a task that makes
possible the more sophisticated treatment he presents in *Strukturen der Lebenswelt*. There is therefore more than merely
historical interest in this study, for it sheds important light both
on Schutz's previous writings and on those that followed.

It is hopefully not out of place in the preface to a manuscript
such as this—preliminary, tentative, still en route, and thus
somewhat personal—to conclude with a few remarks concerning Alfred Schutz himself. As a scholar his reputation is, I think,
firmly established; his writings will continue to be studied and
admired and will come to be even more recognized as the work
of a truly exceptional philosopher and social theorist. But his
stature as a great teacher and remarkably warm and sensitive
human being should also be noted.

Father H. L. van Breda wrote in his Preface to Volume *1* of
Schutz's *Collected Papers,*

> I would like to speak of the man, to evoke the acumen of
> his mind, his penetrating irony, his serenity and courage in
> exile, the wide range of his interests, the gift of youthfulness
> and sympathetic understanding which enabled him to as-
> similate successfully a new culture at the age of forty and to
> become accomplished in it.[18] Fearing to say too little and
> to say it ineptly, I limit myself to recalling his unceasing
> passion to understand man. Schutz was a philosopher, a

18. Schutz was born in Vienna in 1899 and emigrated to the United
States in July 1939, after spending more than a year in Paris when
forced to leave Austria by the coming Nazi occupation.

psychologist, a sociologist, a musicologist; all of these approaches served that passion.[19]

Certainly, those of us who were fortunate enough to have studied under him would enthusiastically endorse this homage. A man of great personal character, bearing, and engaging warmth, Schutz gave unstintingly of himself to his many students, despite the circumstance that in addition to teaching full-time with The Graduate Faculty, he had a more than full-time position as an executive in different corporations simultaneously.[20] Although he always placed himself in the phenomenological tradition of Husserl, he was never a dogmatic and uncritical disciple of Husserl, nor so strapped to the tradition that he saw nothing else. In his teaching and in his writings, in courses and in counsel with students, he constantly insisted on the necessity of serious study of the works of thinkers of every persuasion and discipline. Tolerant and open in the finest philosophical tradition, he had little patience with narrow professionalism, whether educational or philosophical, but at no time did his impatience turn his wonderful sense of humor and irony into ill-tempered sarcasm. He constantly sought out what was common to the divergent currents of thought rather than what separated them. And he himself was expert in his knowledge of the history of philosophy and science, especially in their present-day currents of thought.

Because of the double life he led, all of his studying and writing were done at night, on weekends, and during his infrequent vacations. As Mrs. Schutz expressed it so well in a letter in response to my inquiry,

When we were in Colorado he went every morning on a long walk which led to a beautiful spot surrounded by mountains and meadows. It was a kind of outdoor Lutheran Church

19. Preface, *CP 1*, vi.
20. I am deeply indebted to Mrs. Schutz for learning more of the details and exigencies of Schutz's life and work—exigencies about which many of us students knew only little if anything. Courses at The Graduate Faculty are given at night; hence Prof. Schutz in fact led two full-time careers for most of his life in this country.

and meeting-ground for its members and there were tables and benches. He loved this place dearly and it provided an ideal place for meditating and writing. And there it was where the *Reflections on Relevance* came into being. It certainly wasn't intended to be published in this form. It was a first draft. Every paper he published had been written and re-written many times. And all the papers were destined to be part of his planned book. And the Relevance-manuscript even more so.

His lectures and seminars, too, had this same highly polished and thoroughly conceived form, so strongly did he feel the necessity for exactness and adequacy. His passion for care and precision doubtless stemmed from his "unceasing passion to understand man" which Father van Breda mentions. The urgency of the questions pertaining to the human condition, he felt, demanded thoroughness and breadth of comprehension, or they inevitably become distorted, misunderstood, mere leaves on a bitter wind leading to ineffectual and fanatic actions which only serve to worsen the crisis of modern man.

Mrs. Schutz, too, played a profound role in his life and work,[21] working with the same devotion, care, and patience in seeing that Schutz's lifelong efforts can at least be brought to partial fruition. Certainly her help, encouragement, and patience with my own work on this study have been of decisive importance in its appearance. Partly through her efforts, partly through reading and working with this text and several vol-

---

21. Quite revealing is the following passage from her letter—which with characteristic modesty she describes as "very insignificant": "His book, *Der sinnhafte Aufbau der sozialen Welt,* he dictated to me during many nights and weekends. I took it down in shorthand, typed it and then he worked it over again and again, either again dictating, or writing the next version in longhand, which I transcribed then again into type-written manuscripts [Father van Breda notes that it took twelve years before Schutz regarded this book as finished]. In later years and especially when he wrote in English [whose common vernacular and technical vocabulary Schutz mastered in remarkably short time] he preferred to write every first draft in longhand. I typed it then and he corrected and changed it again, so there were often three or four or even more versions till he finally was satisfied."

umes of lectures which she readily made available to me, and
partly through my own indelible memories of the lively, vividly
humane man himself, I hope to have made this study ring
with the sound of his voice and the great style of his mind:
that his "lifeworld" may come alive for others as it did for us
in the past and be shared by them as he shared with us.

Richard M. Zaner

The University of Texas
February 1969

Having decided to jot down some thoughts on the matter of relevance, I have arranged my writing materials on a table in the garden of my summer house. Starting the first strokes of my pen, I have in my visual field this white sheet of paper, my writing hand, the ink marks forming one line of characters after the other on the white background. Before me is the table with its green surface on which several objects are placed —my pencil, two books, and other things. Further on are the tree and lawn of my garden, the lake with boats, the mountain, and the clouds in the background. I need only turn my head to see the house with its porch, the windows of my room, etc. I hear the buzzing of a motorboat, the voices of the children in the neighbor's yard, the calling of the bird. I experience the kinesthetic movements of my writing hand, I have sensations of warmth, I feel the table supporting my writing arm. All of this is within my perceptual field, a field well organized into spheres of objects: those within my reach, those which once have been within my reach and can be brought within it again, and those which thus far have never been within my reach but which I may bring within it by means of appropriate kinesthetic movements or movements of particular kinds.[2] But none of these

1. In the original table of contents projected for this study, Schutz attached a bracketed note to this section: "Has to be entirely rewritten." In addition to the typewritten version, there is the original handwritten one from which the other was transcribed. Mrs. Ilse Schutz was kind enough to permit me to have access to both for use in developing the present version.

2. For Schutz's analysis of the organization of objects in the field of experience, see his *Collected Papers, 1,* Phaenomenologica 11, (The

perceived things is at the moment thematic for me. My attention is concentrated on a quite specific task (the analysis of the problem of relevance), and my present writing under these and those circumstances is but one among several means by which I could bring about this goal and communicate my thoughts to others.

In the horizon of this thematic field, however, I find not only the perceptual experiences originating in my present spatial position. There is as well my autobiographical situation at the present moment, which is itself but the sedimentation or outcome of my personal history, of all the experiences I have had and which are preserved in my memory or are available within my present stock of knowledge at hand.[3] Included in the latter are not only what I have myself experienced firsthand, but also my socially derived knowledge, which points to the experiences of others (both my contemporaries and my predecessors). For instance, in writing the preceding paragraph, I have in mind the investigations of many others, among them Husserl's far-reaching analysis of a similar phenomenon, William James' pertinent inquiries, Bergson's theories of the pragmatic function of memory, the doctrines of the Gestaltists, Aron Gurwitsch's theory of the field of consciousness (as he explained it to me in many conversations), Ludwig Landgrebe's paper on inner and outer horizons, the sociological theory of "definition of situations," many talks I have had with friends on all these matters, and, surely, all my own previous thoughts dealing

---

Hague, Martinus Nijhoff, 1962), "Symbol, Reality and Society," 287–356, esp. 306–11 and 326–29. (References to this *Collected Papers*, Vols. *1, 2* [Phaenomenologica 15, 1964], and *3* [Phaenomenologica 22, 1966], will be cited as *CP 1, CP 2,* and *CP 3,* respectively, along with the specific essay referred to.)

3. For Schutz's conception of the stock of knowledge at hand, see below, Ch. 3, Sec. E, and Ch. 5. See also *CP 1,* "Common-Sense and Scientific Interpretation of Human Action," 3–47; and his *The Phenomenology of the Social World* (Evanston, Northwestern University Press, 1967), pp. 80–81. (References to the latter book, a translation from the 2nd edition of *Der sinnhafte Aufbau der sozialen Welt* [Vienna, Springer-Verlag, 1960], will be cited as *PSW.)*

with the problem at hand (toward whose clarification and unification the present effort is directed).[4]

On the other hand, the social background of my present
writing enters into this horizon. For example, living in an
English-speaking country, I have chosen the English language
as my scheme of expression. My act of writing is determined, in
part, by the expectation that others, using this language as their
scheme of interpretation, might become readers of what I
write. I am writing these lines, moreover, during my vacation;
that is, I anticipate my return to professional duties (and all
that this entails), and this socioeconomic determination of my
present situation, too, is in the horizon of my present activity.
Nevertheless, it is only the investigation of the problem at hand
which is now thematic for me, and the field of perceptions, of
autobiographical recollections, of social relationships, of socioeconomic determination, and so on, forms merely the horizon
of this activity upon which I am concentrated.

The first object of our analysis is the field of consciousness,

4. The studies to which Schutz refers here are: Edmund Husserl,
*Ideen zu einer reinen Phänomenologie und phänomenologischen Philo-
sophie* (Halle a.d.S., Max Niemeyer, 1913) (later included in *Husserliana*, Band III [The Hague, Martinus Nijhoff, 1950]; Eng. trans. by
W. R. Boyce Gibson [New York, Macmillan, 1931]) (further references
to this work will be cited as *Ideen 1*); Husserl, *Formale und transzen-
dentale Logik* (Halle a.d.S., Max Niemeyer, 1929), Sec. 74, (an English
translation of this work by Dorion Cairns is to be published soon);
Husserl, *Erfahrung und Urteil*, edited by L. Landgrebe (Hamburg,
Claassen Verlag, 1954), Secs. 24, 51b, 58, 61 (an English translation of
this work by Robert Jordan is in progress); William James, *Principles of
Psychology* (2 vol. New York, Henry Holt & Co., 1890); Henri Bergson,
Matière et mémoire (Paris, Presses Universitaires de France, 1939), esp.
Ch. 2 *(Matter and Memory* [London, Allen and Unwin, 1911]); Aron
Gurwitsch, *Théorie du champ de la conscience* (Paris, Desclée de
Brouwer, 1957), esp. Parts I, III, V, VI *(The Field of Consciousness*
[Pittsburgh, Duquesne University Press, 1964]); Ludwig Landgrebe,
"The World As A Phenomenological Problem," tr. Dorion Cairns,
Philosophy and Phenomenological Research, 1, (1940), 38–58. Con-
cerning Schutz's treatment of W. I. Thomas' notion of the "definition
of situation," cf. *CP 1*, "Common-Sense and Scientific Interpretation
of Human Action," 9, and "Concept and Theory Formation in the
Social Sciences," esp. 54.

insofar as it is structured into a thematic kernel which stands
out over against a surrounding horizon and is given at any
"now" of inner duration. Husserl has investigated the functions
of what he calls the "attentional ray" for the constitution of the
thematic kernel and therewith for the structurization of the
whole field.[5] At any moment there are many experiences going
on simultaneously. What constitutes one (or better, one strain)
of these temporally ongoing and simultaneous experiences as
the thematic one is the fact that I voluntarily turn to it or reflect
upon it (and hence this is an ego-activity, insofar as the ego
is the source of all the activities of my conscious life).[6] Husserl's
description of this activity may lead to the misconception that
this selection, this choice, may be performed at random within
an unlimited range of freedom or discretion. Indeed, Sartre
(who invariably likes to give his theories the appearance of
legitimacy by referring them to Husserl, whom he has nevertheless not understood) bases his philosophy of freedom of the
involved "for-itself" *(le pour soi engagé)* on the contention that
man is at every moment and in every circumstance free to make
thematic whatever experience he pleases, adding that man is
condemned to such freedom.[7] This is certainly not Husserl's
meaning. The activities of consciousness and the ego's attentional ray—this "turning-to" and "turning-away-from" certain
experiences which makes them thematic or nonthematic, i.e.
horizonal[8]—takes place within a very restricted scope of dis-

5. Cf. Husserl, *Ideen 1*, Secs. 77–79, 92.
6. Cf. Husserl, *Cartesianische Meditationen, Husserliana* I (The
Hague, Martinus Nijhoff, 1950), Meditation IV *(Cartesian Meditations*,
tr. Dorion Cairns [The Hague, Martinus Nijhoff, 1960]); also, *Ideen 1*,
Secs. 35, 37, 57, 80.
7. Cf. Sartre, *L'Être et le néant* (Paris, Librairie Gallimard 1943),
pp. 513–14 *(Being and Nothingness*, tr. Hazel Barnes [New York,
Philosophical Library, 1956], pp. 439–40); and Schutz, *CP 1*, "Sartre's
Theory of the Alter Ego," 180–206.
8. On the phenomenological notion of "horizons," see Landgrebe,
"The World As A Phenomenological Problem"; Husserl, *Ideen 1*, Secs.
82, 113, 114; Husserl, *Erfahrung und Urteil*, Secs. 8–10; Schutz, *CP 1*,
"Some Leading Concepts of Phenomenology," 99–117, esp. 108 f.;
Schutz, *CP 3*, "Type and Eidos in Husserl's Late Philosophy," esp. 98 f.;
Gurwitsch, *The Field of Consciousness*, pp. 234–46; and Helmut Kuhn,

realms appear "irreal" and only derived from that receiving this accent.[13]

Each of these multiple realities, or finite provinces of meaning, has its own degree of tension of consciousness and *attention à la vie*. Each may be reached from any other one by a modification of either of the latter—a modification which is subjectively experienced as a shock or leap.[14] It therefore seems that the bestowal of the accent of reality upon any of these provinces, the alteration of the tension of consciousness from wide-awakeness through all the various degrees up to deep sleep, is the first step leading to the determination of the field of consciousness itself—including the thematic kernel and its surrounding horizon, as it is given at any moment of our inner time.

From among all these virtual realms of reality, or finite provinces of meaning, we wish to focus on that of working acts in the outer world (that realm in which alone things can be, and which is subject to changes caused by our bodily movements). Attention is thus restricted to the general problem of the theme and horizon pertaining to that state of full-awakeness characteristic of this realm. But this focusing and restricting is itself an illustration of our topic: this particular realm of reality, this province among all the other provinces, is declared to be

13. While engaged in a context of concern, action, and thought such as in a game, other concerns (e.g. those pertaining to one's scientific activity) are not brought into play, they are irrelevant to the province of the game; the overt performance (working) of raising one's arm and grasping an object, while seemingly "the same" in two contexts of action, are different performances precisely inasmuch as they occur within different contexts. Other concerns do not disappear; they are not "unreal" but merely "irreal."

14. The movement from one context of concern ("finite province of meaning"), with all of its appurtenant relevancies, activities, attitudes, norms, etc., to another (e.g. awakening from a dream, or moving from "study" to the everyday concern of eating) is experienced as a kind of shock, a leap. Cf. *CP 1*, "On Multiple Realities," 231 f., where Schutz emphasizes the connection of this to different tensions of consciousness and *attention à la vie*. Aron Gurwitsch has given a sensitive critical appraisal of Schutz's theory of relevance and finite provinces of meaning; cf. *The Field of Consciousness*, pp. 394–404.

the paramount reality and made, so to speak, thematic in the research of these philosophers (namely, Bergson and James)— a move which renders all the other provinces surrounding this thematic kernel merely horizonal (and most unclarified as well). But the structurization into theme and horizon is basic to the mind, and to explain that kind of structure by confusing what is founded on it with its founding principle is a true *petitio principii* indeed.

In the next place, these various provinces or realms of reality are interconnected by the unity of my own mind, which may at any time extend or compress its tension by turning to and away from life—by changing, in Bergson's phrase, its attention to life (this term to be understood here as life within paramount reality). Closer inspection, however, shows that I, this psycho-physiological unity, live in several of these realms simultaneously.[15] My writing of these lines is a series of working acts in the outer world, acts which change it by the ink strokes produced on this sheet of paper. But at the same time I am involved in theoretical contemplation in the effort to organize and articulate my thoughts on the problem at hand. In terms of this prevailing interest, my working activity is merely secondary, that is to say, a means by which to give these thoughts a kind of permanence for myself (so that I may return to them in further reflection) and eventually to make them communicable to others. The levels of my personality involved in both of these simultaneously performed activities are of different degrees of intimacy—they are different as regards their respective nearness or distance to what is most intimately the core of my personality. The experienced innervation of my writing hand belongs to the vital sphere, and the writing act itself goes on unperturbed so long as there are no inner or outer obstacles (such as aches in my fingers, difficulties with my pen or with the paper, and the like), and thus it is so to speak automatized. At the same time, there is that level of the act of putting down my thoughts which goes beyond the immediacies of writing: finding the adequate words, arranging these sentences, adding

15. See below, Ch. 5, Sec. B (2) and (3).

these to other sentences forming paragraphs, and so on—all of these reproducing step by step the many articulations of my thought. Nevertheless, despite the complexity, the process of translating my thought into language goes on unattended and almost automatic, so long as there is no hitch which compels me to stop and put my scheme of expression (in the present case, the English language) itself into question—as might happen, for example, as regards the adequacy of a term used for expressions of what I mean, or as to the correct application of the syntactical rules immanent to this expressional scheme, to the polythetic steps of my thinking.

But the activity upon which I am really concentrated, this activity of a purely internal nature, this inner-performance of mine to investigate the problem at hand in a step-by-step analysis, is, as a matter of fact, independent of all those acts concomitantly performed. The theme of my present conscious field would remain thematic under quite different circumstances—as when I am taking a walk, lying in bed, or paddling a canoe. And the activity connected with the translating of this thought into English language is the same whether I am talking or writing or even merely using this idiom in an "internal dialogue," namely, as when I formulate it in my thought silently. Finally, I may bring this formulated thought to paper by using shorthand or longhand or typing, and each of these activities require other innervations, other changes in the outer world, other visual impressions received from both the visible movements of my writing hand and the outcome of this activity, the signs with which this sheet of paper has been covered. Consequently, it was my choice to make longhand writing thematic in this sphere of outer activity by using the so-called Roman alphabet. It was my choice to use the English language (with all its syntactical rules and terminological implications for the purposes of articulating my thought). It was my choice to do my thinking on the problems involved here by trying to write it down, pen in hand, instead of thinking it over during a walk—that is, to make this "this-pen-in-hand" the theme of my activity. And finally, it was my choice to make thematic for my contemplating performance a study of the problem of theme and horizon itself (instead of, say, a study on the Greek skeptics). What I am now engaged in doing—"writing-in-English-in-longhand-a-paper-on-the-problem-of-relevance"—is certainly experienced by me as a unity. Thinking through the problem of relevance is the theme of my activity, but this activity is spread over several realms or levels of my conscious life, each with its own particular tension, its particular dimension of time, its particular articulations into thematic kernel and horizonal surrounding. Despite the temporal substructurization pertaining to each of these sphere and dimensions, I live in them all simultaneously. Thus, although I spend but an hour at my desk, I traverse within this measurable period of outer time an ongoing span of my inner life which condenses experiences, skills, and knowledge acquired in the greater part of my lifetime into the writing down of a single page.

Although experienced as a unity, what I am doing is not one single activity; it is rather a set of heterogeneous activities, each of them taking place in its own appropriate medium. This set of activities is itself structurized into theme and horizon. In our case, the performance of the analysis, the contemplation of the problem of relevance, is thematic and all the other activities horizonal. It is the predominance of the theme which creates the apparent unification of this set of activities, and it bestows the main accent of reality upon the realm of theoretical contemplation. Seen from this perspective all the other activities simultaneously performed in other dimensions seem to be not irreal but subordinate and ancillary. To be sure, this apparently unified activity may break asunder at any moment: I have to consult a dictionary, I must remove a scrap from my pen, and so on. In such an event the topic of my thought, the theme of this chain of activities, will have to be abandoned; its flux will be interrupted. I have to "turn-away" from it and "turn-toward" an activity performed on quite another level and pertaining to quite another realm (such as cleaning my pen).

It was therefore an oversimplification to state as we did that we are living in different provinces of reality which we can interchange by a leap from one to another, and that the selection of one of them is the first step toward defining what is thematic and what is merely horizonal in our field of consciousness. In truth we are always living and acting simultaneously in several of these provinces, and to select one can merely mean that we are making it so to speak our "home base," "our system of reference," our paramount reality in relation to which all others receive merely the accent of derived reality—namely, they become horizonal, ancillary, subordinate in relation to what is the prevailing theme. But these terms themselves express and presuppose the categories of relevance—of the theme-field relation, therefore—and we find ourselves again in the face of a *petitio principii*.

The corollary to the fact that we live simultaneously in various provinces of reality or meaning is the fact that we put into play various levels of our personality—and this indicates a hidden reference to the *schizophrenic-ego hypothesis*.[16] The delimitation of the field itself (and within the delimited field the structurization into thematic kernel and surrounding horizonal levels) is itself a function of the level of our personality involved. Only very superficial levels of our personality are involved in such performances as our habitual and even quasi-automatic "household chores," or eating, dressing, and (for normal adults) also in reading and performing simple arithmetical operations. To be sure, when we turn to such routine work, the activities connected with it are constituted as thematic, requiring and receiving our full attention if only momentarily. But we may perform these activities in the midst of and in spite of the greatest crises of our lives. Our fear or happiness with respect to a particular event, involving deep levels of our personality, may appear merely horizonal while we are attending to such routine work. But this is mere appearance. The fear or happiness which is thematic for the deeper level of our personality has never been "released from our grip,"[17] we have

16. See below, Ch. 5.
17. This phrase is derived from Husserl's lectures on inner time consciousness, in which he shows that every phase of the "stream" of con-

never really turned away from it, we have not and could not interrupt it in order to pay attention to it again tomorrow. It has been temporarily relegated into the horizon by a voluntary and sometimes even painful act of willpower; or better, we have pulled the routine work into the thematical foreground and pushed what was hitherto thematic into the background. So at least it seems. What actually happens in such a case is that two different levels of our personality (a superficial and a deeper one) are simultaneously involved, the theme of the activities of one of them being reciprocally the horizon of the other. Because of this, the "actualized" theme received a specific tinge from the other, the temporarily covert one, which remains so to speak the hidden ground determining the occurrences in the clearly discernible voices founded upon it.

But this metaphor is not quite adequate and should be replaced by another one, expressly borrowed from the structure of music. What I have in mind is the relationship between two independent themes simultaneously going on in the same flux or flow of music; or, more briefly, the relationship of counterpoint. The listener's mind may pursue one or the other, take one as the main theme and the other as the subordinate one, or vice versa: one determines the other, and nevertheless it remains predominant in the intricate web of the whole structure. It is this "counterpointal structure" of our *personality* and therewith of our stream of consciousness which is the corollary of what has been called in other connections the *schizophrenic hypothesis of the ego*—namely the fact that in order to make something thematic and another thing horizonal we have to assume an artificial split of the unity of our personality. There are merely two activities of our personality, if contemplated in isolation,

---

sciousness is essentially and automatically (passively) *retentional:* immediately past phases of some present phase are "still held in grip" (*noch-im-Griff-halten* or *-haben*) within the structure of the present phase. Schutz uses the phrase in a wider sense, however, to characterize "ego-activity" (*Ich-Akte*) as well as the sphere of automaticity (*Passivität*). Cf. Husserl, *The Phenomenology of Inner-Time Consciousness,* tr. James S. Churchill (Bloomington, Indiana University Press, 1967), pp. 40–97.

where the distinction into theme and horizon seems to be a more or less clean-cut one; that is on the one hand, for example, perceiving phenomena in the outer world and, on the other hand, "working," that is changing this outer world by means of bodily movements. But further investigation will show that even in these cases the theory concerning the mind's selective activity is simply the title for a set of problems more complicated even than those of field, theme, and horizon—namely, a title for the basic phenomenon we suggest calling *relevance*. But before we turn to this study, a word on certain special cases of personality structure might be indicated.

We do not intend to consider here the pathological cases of split personality or schizophrenia in the psychiatrical sense, nor phenomena such as aphasia or apraxia which prevent certain levels of personality from entering into play. The modern psychoanalytic theory of the subconscious has to be considered, not as a solution of the epistemological or philosophical problems involved, as many followers of the doctrine pretend, but insofar as the so-called subconscious is connected with the problem at hand: that is, the relationship between theme and field on the one hand and the theory of relevance on the other.

It has been frequently maintained that Leibniz' *theory of small perceptions* (which although perceived are nevertheless not apperceived) was a precursor of the doctrines of Freud. According to Leibniz, as is well known, these small unapperceived perceptions motivate and determine those of our actions which are not subject to voluntary choice. They are omnipresent; that is, changing as they are, they constitute the background of our consciousness. In terms of the phenomenological language of field and horizon, it is more than a merely terminological question whether we may include these small perceptions in the concepts of the field and horizon of consciousness. What is within the field can be virtually apperceived. Anything within the horizon, moreover, can be made a theme of our thought. But Leibniz' "small perceptions" cannot be made a theme because according to him they can be apperceived merely "en masse"; but any single small perception is, by definition, indiscernible from any other. They are, as a whole, comparable to the breakers of the sea. We may apperceive the murmur of the surf but not the sound of the single waves entering into it, because they are indiscernible, they never have been and never could become thematic.

It seems a precondition of any thematization that the experience constituting this theme has its own history of which it is the sedimentation. Any one of these experiences inherently refers to previous experiences from which it is derived and to which it refers. I am, thus, at any time in a position to question any of these as to its genesis or historical origin. In other words, each theme refers to elements which formerly have been within the field of our consciousness, either as a former theme or at least as horizonal and thus virtually thematizable. Neither is the case with respect to small perceptions.

The content of what Freud calls *subconscious life,* however, can be virtually thematized, and the analytical technique consists first in bringing the hidden motive of the neurotic behavior into the horizonal field of consciousness, and finally making it its thematic kernel. To the patient, his neurotic behavior with its undisclosed motive is the theme related to an outer level of his personaliy. The hidden counterpart in a deeper level of his personality is thematically concerned with what psychoanalytical terminology has baptized the "subconscious motive" of such behavior. But it is subconscious only if the manifest behavior has been taken as the paramount field (and this is frequently done because the manifestations are those occurring in the realm of paramount reality constituted by working acts in the outer world).[18]

Here, for the first time in the course of our investigation, we discover a main topic of later chapters: namely, the fact that field, theme, horizon, and relevance have an entirely different structure when viewed subjectively (that is, from the point of view of the subject in question) and objectively (that is, seen from an observer's point of view). The reason for this is pre-

18. That is, the province of everyday life as it is for our "wide-awake" experiences.

cisely the counterpointal structure of our personality and our stream of consciousness itself. Living *simultaneously* in various realms of reality, in various tensions of consciousness and modes of *attention à la vie,* in various dimensions of time, putting into play different levels of our personality (or different degrees of anonymity and intimacy), the counterpointal articulation of the themes and horizons pertaining to each of such levels (including finally the schizophrenic patterns of the ego) are all *expressions of the single basic phenomenon: the interplay of relevance structures.*

The *psychoanalytic technique* itself seems to confirm this interpretation: the *"free association"* which the patient is invited to perform leads to an oscillating of the thematic field at random from one level of the personality to another. Thus dreams, pertaining to thematic experiences in the realm of reality opposite to the full-awakeness of the pragmatic world of working, are made the key of the interpretation of fields pertaining to entirely different realms of relevance. So, too, free phantasies. But all the experiences which analysis brings about have at one time been actual or virtual themes of our conscious life; that is, they have been historically (autobiographically) either within the horizon or even within the kernel of our past fields of consciousness. The role of the "selective capacity of our memory" becomes especially important in this regard. We will have to deal with it separately later on. But the relegation of themes into the subconscious seems to confirm Bergson's statement that the real enigma involved in the phenomenon of memory is not what we remember but what we forget.[19]

19. Cf. Bergson, *Matière et mémoire,* pp. 133–56 (pp. 152–81).

A. The Concept of the πιθανόν *and its Modifications*

In order to study the problem of relevance in the sphere of perception, we may remember, as Jankélévitch pointed out in his book *L'Alternative*,[1] that *any perception itself involves the problem of choice*. We have to choose within the perceptual field those elements which may become in Husserl's terminology thematic and subject to "interpretations." Such interpretations do not necessarily have the form of predicative judgments. The passive syntheses of recognition, similarity, identity, dissimilarity, likeness, and so on,[2] are interpretative events happening in the prepredicative sphere. The recognition of an object as the same or as the same but modified, or the recognition of its modification, are the outcome of such prepredicative syntheses. In his book *Erfahrung und Urteil,* Hus-

1. Vladimir Jankélévitch, *L'Alternative* (Paris, F. Alcan, 1938).
2. That is, those continuously ongoing temporal syntheses by virtue of which we experience an object as the same (or different) through multiple awareness of it (or through multiple phases of a single awareness of it). These syntheses, for Husserl, occur continuously without any ego-activity, or even ego-advertence, being necessary. Only in this sense are they "passive" or, better, "automatic" (Dorion Cairns' suggested translation, meant to emphasize that Husserl's notion of passivity is in no sense the traditional empiricist one). The term "prepredicative" designates those subjective processes of consciousness *(Erlebnisse)* that are not characterized by the presence of the ego (in which the ego does not "live," or is not "busied" with their respective "objects")—i.e. the term is synonymous with the sphere of passivity. Cf. Husserl, *Cartesian Meditations*, Secs. 17–18, 38–39, 51–52; also *Ideen 1,* Secs. 97–127.

serl has studied various cases of such *prepredicative interpreta-tions* which may or may not be verified or falsified by further experiences.[3] He is especially interested in the problems of alternatives in which several interpretations of the same percept compete with one another. In case of such competing he calls them *problematic possibilities;* each of them stands to choice, as it were. Each has its own weight, and the mind oscillates from the one to the other weighing these possibilities before it comes to a decision—a decision which itself is always open to verifica-tion or falsification by even further events.[4]

Husserl's theory may be correlated to Bergson's *interpreta-tion of choice,* found in the last chapter of *Time and Free Will.*[5] According to Bergson, it is not the case that there are two pos-sibilities standing to choice. He speaks therefore not of choos-ing between two possible interpretations or courses of action, but of two ways of possible action or two goals to be brought about before any such process of choosing. There are not two goals and two ways before the mind has established the former and drafted the latter. When this is done, the mind oscillates between both of them, dropping one and returning to the other until the decision separates itself from the mind as a ripe fruit falls from a tree. It is obviously this Bergsonian concept of the alternative which has influenced Jankélévitch in constructing his aforementioned theory.

Interesting as these modern theories are, it seems that the most careful analysis of the phenomenon in question here has been made by the Greek skeptical philosopher Carneades in his theory of the πιθανόν (in Latin, *probabile;* we here follow Robin's presentation).[6] The term πιθανόν has to be translated

3. Cf. Husserl, *Erfahrung und Urteil,* Secs. 8, 22, 24, 25, 26, 80, and esp. 83 (a) and (b).

4. For Husserl's notion of "problematic possibilities" see *Ideen 1,* Secs. 105 and 106.

5. Cf. Bergson, *Essai sur les données immédiates de la conscience* (Paris, Presses Universitaires de France, 1927), pp. 129–53, esp. pp. 132–37 *(Time and Free Will* [London, Allen and Unwin, 1910], pp. 172–204, esp. pp. 175–83).

6. Schutz notes the report of Carneades' doctrines by Sextus Em-piricus, *Adversus Logicus, 7,* and by Cicero in the first *Academica.* He

sometimes by "probable" and sometimes by "permissive," but the term "plausible" will render most exactly the meaning of the Greek term.

Carneades begins his analysis of this notion with a polemic against its use by the Stoics, especially Chrysippos, who classified all representations *(phantasiae, vira)* into those which are and those which are not plausible, subdividing each of these categories into those which are true, false, or neither true nor false. Denying the possibility of grasping truth, Carneades rejects this classification. According to him it is necessary to distinguish between what is not known to us (the ἀκατάληπτον, the "incomprehensible," and what is uncertain ἄδηλον, *incertum).* There is no truth as such; there are merely problematic truths, true for us, in us, and by us. *Not verity but verisimilitude* is what we can hope for, the latter term meaning not what is similar to verity, but what seems to me to be verity—to me, in the specific condition in which I find myself and which consequently has the chance of not being contradicted or denied by other representations. This is, of course, quite a different concept from that of the *comprehensible representation* (φαντασία καταλήπτικα) of the Stoics, that is, the representation which "sees" the represented things as they are, and which alone can govern the conduct of the sage.

The skeptic understands, however, that the sage, too, is a human being, and that his truth is merely human truth. He is not sculptured from stone nor cut out from wood. He has a soul, a mind, a body which moves around. All his impressions, perceptions, knowledge are referred to and dependent upon his humanity. As a sage he will suspend judgment on the true nature of things; he will adopt the attitude of ἐποχή (an ἐποχή in Greek which, although having given the name to ἐποχή of phenomenological reduction, must not be confused with the latter). But for his practical action he will not look for guidance to "comprehensible representations" which, as he knows, are

---

also refers to the "brilliant presentation" by Léon Robin, *Pyrrhon et le scepticisme greque* (Paris, Presses Universitaires de France, 1944).

unattainable. If he contemplates a voyage at sea, he does not know exactly what this voyage will be like. But although it is unknown (ἀκατάληπτον) to him how his project will materialize, it is by no means uncertain (ἄδηλον): if he chooses a good vessel, a reliable captain, and if the weather is favorable, he *thinks,* to be sure, that he will arrive safely at the port of his destination. It is this sort of representation upon which the sage of Carneades bases his acting or his refraining from acting, which he adopts as *concilia agendi ad non agendi,* as Cicero formulates this principle. *Notwithstanding his epistemological skepticism* he will therefore, *in the sphere of his actions, weigh his motives* which determine his judgments and acts (πιθαναί, from which πιθανόν). To him, certitude is a mere belief having its own motives and causes: the motives being assignable reasons in intelligible terms; the causes, that is reasons, not assignable in such terms being our passion, prejudices, habit, constraint exercised by social and family groups, and the like. The opposite of certitude is uncertitude, but this opposition is not of a contradictory nature; between complete incertitude or radical doubt and sufficient certitude or armored belief, there is a full gamut of intermediary positions. Certitude has its degrees, and Carneades has elaborated a typology of some of them.

He starts with the observation that there is no pure representation existing in our mind. If I am thinking of Socrates, for example, I do not think merely of the name of Socrates, but along with this I think of some of his individual characteristics, his conduct, and other circumstances which cannot be separated from his existence. If my actual representation did not contain a sufficient number of such elements composing the individual in question, or if it contained those incompatible with the former, I would in fact believe that I am not thinking of Socrates but rather of some other person. What now are the degrees of certainty in such a case? (1) There is first of all simple likelihood (probability); that is, there is the "same possibility" for one solution or for its contrary. The example given by Sextus is the following: I am persecuted by my enemies and

I see a ditch where I might find a place to hide from them. But I might be mistaken. Who knows whether or not some of my enemies are themselves hidden in this ditch? I have no time to verify whether my qualms are well founded and it would be imprudent to do so; thus I do not know whether I am right or wrong in being distrustful. But under these circumstances, everything else being equal, it will *probably* be better to look for refuge elsewhere. (2) Hercules brings Alkestis back from the underworld and leads her before Admetos: a case of true representation. He therefore does not believe in his actual representation of a living Alkestis. This representation is "pulled in a contrary sense," it became "bent" (better: "twisted," περίσπαστος)—it is *stricken out,* as Husserl would say. Without his previous knowledge, Admetos would believe in what he sees. His representation would remain unbent (ἀπερίπαστος), which would bestow upon it a higher degree of certitude than simple probability.

(3) The verified representation (in the more exact sense of this term) presupposes that the simple probability and the "unbent" probability have already been ascertained. The verification adds one reason more for being convinced—for being "certain." It is the most perfect modality of discrimination between what is believable and what is not. The example given of this is: During the wintertime a man suddenly enters a poorly illuminated room and observes in a corner a pile of rope. He sees the thing, but not clearly. Is it really a pile of rope or is it a serpent? Either is equally possible—reason enough for the man to distrust his first interpretation (this is the first stage comparable to the "simple probability" of our first case, which defines the "problematic alternative" in Husserl's meaning). The man now becomes uneasy; his thought oscillates between one and the other of the two possible alternatives. Approaching the object he thinks that it is a rope: it does not move, and so on. On the other hand, he "comes to think of it" that the color of serpents is very similar to that of rope and that in wintertime serpents, made rigid by the cold, do not move. He therefore moves around his representation (περιοδεύειν, περιόδενοις)

without coming to a solution because each of the alternatives
has its own weight, one balances the other. He is not able to
give his assent (συγκατάθεσις, *assensus*) to the one or the other
by virtue of mere logical reasons, but it may depend upon his
courage or his timidity whether he will believe in the one or in
the other; whether, in the language of Carneades, one of them
will become περίπαστος or ἀπερίπαστος, or, in Husserl's language, one of them will be stricken out and the other prevail
(this is the second stage of his deliberation). If he is inclined
to believe that he erroneously assumed the object to be dangerous, he may feel the need to obtain a higher degree of
certitude. He will look for proof, and doing so, he will as Sextus
says employ the method of the Athenian authorities in *examin-
ing the title and rights of a candidate to public office or of a
physician in diagnosing the illness of a patient.* In other words,
he will not stick to one or several symptoms but will take into
account all the tokens ("syndromes") observed concurrently.
If, in the bundle of syndromes concurrently observed, there is
no representation which may constitute a counterindication or
an indication of a possible error, then he will say that the representation adopted by him is true. Thus, the man may take a
stick and hit the object, but it still does not move: "No, surely
this is not a serpent." With this last proof he has completed *in
detail* the tour around his representation (διεξοδεύειν, διέξοδος),
and he may establish giving his now well-founded assent or
conviction that he was mistaken to think that the object was a
serpent. Thus, in the διέξοδος, in the methodical control of the
nature and degree of the probabilities (πιθανόν), consists the
only valid criterion of our opinions.

B. *Husserl's Concept of Problematic Possibilities and the Field of the Unproblematic*

The similarity of Carneades' theory of the πιθανόν and its
degrees with Husserl's analysis of problematic possibilities in
Erfahrung und Urteil is conspicuous. Professor Robin, from
whose lucid book we have amply borrowed, discusses the ques-

tion whether Carneades' theory as outlined is meant to refer
exclusively to the realm of action, as many have believed, or to
all kinds of cogitations such as judgments, perceptions, and so
on. And by comparing the texts and qualifying their contents,
he comes to affirm the latter hypothesis. This again squares with
Husserl's analysis—according to which the source of problematic possibilities is rooted in the prepredicative sphere.

But whereas for Carneades these problematic possibilities
are apparently restricted to all kinds of *activities* of the mind
(although not merely to actions in the sense of working acts
gearing into the outer world), it appears that Husserl cannot
disregard their reference to the passive synthesis by which,
according to him, relations such as sameness, likeness, and so
on, are constituted. It is this passive synthesis[7] that relates
actual experiences to data already experienced[8] which data,
in the form of types, are elements of our stock of knowledge at
hand. By means of the passive synthesis of recognition, actual
experiences are matched with or superimposed upon the types
of the already experienced material. Thus objectively they will
or will not then prove to be congruent; they will resemble or
differ from one another. Subjectively we may identify an actual
experience with something already experienced as the "same,"
or the "same but modified," or a "like one"; we may "recognize" it or find out that there is nothing within the stock of our
previously typified knowledge congruent or even comparable
with the actual one—and then we will acknowledge this actual
experience as novel, that is, as one which cannot be matched
with something already experienced by means of the passive
synthesis of recognition.

However, important as this problem is for a general theory of

7. The synthesis referred to here is what Husserl calls the "synthesis of identification." Cf. *Cartesian Meditations,* Secs. 15–17.
8. Schutz's term is "pre-experienced data," which, however, does
not denote something *not* experienced (or something *before* any experience), but rather what has already been experienced. I have therefore
chosen throughout such English expressions as "previously experienced," which do not have the ambiguity and awkwardness of "pre-
experienced."

experience—and we shall have to take it up later on—it is not at the center of our interests in investigating the relationship between theme and horizon, the selective function of the mind, and the underlying structure of relevance. Still, all of these theories—those of Carneades, Husserl, Bergson, Jankélévitch —have in common the assumption that within the given field of our consciousness, several configurations (perceptual or fancied or otherwise) compete with one another for our interpretative assent. They compete in the manner of problematic possibilities or alternatives: each has a certain appeal to us, each has its particular weight, each is capable of being connected with previous experiences, at least as to the type inherent to them. So to speak, at the moment preceding our *periodeusis* we have in the field of our consciousness an unstructurized whole of contiguous configurations, each of which is capable of becoming theme or remaining as horizon within this field.

The situation is therefore different from that which is at the beginning of Gestalt psychology's inquiry. The Gestaltist, too, assumes as given an unstructurized common field and seeks to prove that by an act of interpretation the selective capacity of the mind structurizes this field into what is background and what stands out (that is, it is the Gestalt) from such a background. But he does not show how, within this unstructurized field (which is, to use Husserl's term, a field of open possibilities, a mere open frame within which all kinds of interpretational structurization may become equally valid, all of them having equal weight and equal appeal, all of them competing with all the others), the genuine alternative, that of the problematic possibilities, might be constituted. The Gestalt to be interpretatively delimited within the open field (or better, the several configurations which in the process of oscillating are made in turn theme and horizon within the open field) is from the outset privileged. I may have a choice to interpret this or that configuration as the Gestalt or as belonging to the background of the field; but this is possible only if, within the field itself, not one but several interpretative possibilities have been constituted as problematic ones.

Within the first degree of the $\pi\iota\theta\alpha\nu\acute{o}\nu$ (that is, mere likelihood), any kind of interpretation, any relationship to typical, previously experienced data, is equally possible. Each of the configurations "selected" within this field may become thematic or horizonal, and it is as a matter of principle quite immaterial whether this process is due to a passive synthesis as Husserl assumes or to an act of choosing and comparing as apparently Jankélévitch presupposes. But how then do we explain the second stage of the interpretative procedure—that which Carneades designates as the struggle between *perispastos* and *aperispastos* representations, or in Husserl's terms between the problematic possibilities? To form the question in different terms, how and by what procedure are some of the open possibilities selected and matched and thus converted into problematic possibilities, each of which has its $\pi\iota\theta\alpha\nu\acute{o}\nu$ (likelihood) and nevertheless is brought together by the relationship of $\pi\epsilon\rho\acute{\iota}\sigma\pi\alpha\sigma\tau\sigma\varsigma$ or $\dot{\alpha}\pi\epsilon\rho\acute{\iota}\sigma\pi\alpha\sigma\tau\sigma\varsigma$? What makes the man in Carneades' example oscillate between interpreting the something in the dark corner of the room as either a pile of rope or a serpent? It may even be open to many other interpretations: it might be a heap of stones, or a bundle of laundry, or what not. In his actual situation—it is winter, the room is badly illuminated, he is pusillanimous—he is not interested in inquiries of such a kind. His interest is rather in learning whether this object is dangerous and this requires certain measures to be taken, certain actions to be performed. Here is an object in the corner of the room that is within his unstructuralized field of visual perception. Why, first of all, does this object appeal to his attention to such an extent that he makes it the theme of his interpreting activity? What makes the interpretation of this object at all a problem to him? There may be many other objects in this room, perhaps in other corners, perhaps in the same corner of the room, which leave him entirely indifferent; yet they are all within his unstructuralized field of vision. They remain in the horizon. They do not become, in his actual situation, thematic. They present no problem, interpretative or otherwise, and he thus does not "pay attention" to them. This something which he will attempt to interpret either as a pile of rope or as a serpent is, in some way, privileged among all the other objects in the room. It stands out over against them, it is from the outset—to introduce this term by anticipating later results—*relevant* to him. This may have the most different reasons, and in order to specify these we should have to have full knowledge not only of the situational elements in the present autobiographical moment of the man, but of all the history, the antecedent genesis which leads to this actual situation (in other words, of all the sedimentations of which the actual situation is the outcome). It might be, for instance, that the room the man is entering is his own room with which he is completely familiar, all the details of which are well known to him—known in the sense of passive or automatic habitual knowledge in the familiarity of routine experience. He then expects upon entering to find his room more or less as he left it, to find it again unchanged as he has found it many times when he returned to his house: his home, of which he cannot think otherwise than under the idealization of "again the same."

This set of expectations may constitute the unclarified but pertinent frame of all possible experiences of the room he expects to have when entering it at this specific moment. But this set of expectations, *this field of the unproblematic* which constitutes or at least coconstitutes the frame of reference of all possible experiences he expects to have, proves to be broken asunder by a novel experience having neither the mark of the unproblematic nor that of familiarity. In a single glance he discovers within the hitherto unbroken field of his visual perception an element which does not correspond to what he expected —this something in the corner. What might it be? Why is it unfamiliar? Why does it not fit into the expected field of the unproblematic which he routinely supposed he would find again? The man might have entered the room thematically concerned with quite another topic—say, for example, he was thinking of his friends or of his forthcoming trip. But the collapse of his expectations, the unexpected change, *imposes* upon him a change of his thematic field. Something which was sup-

posed to be familiar and therefore unproblematic proves to be
unfamiliar. It thus has to be investigated and ascertained as to
its nature; it became problematic and thus has to be made into
a theme and not left in the indifference of the concomitant
horizonal background. It is sufficiently relevant to be imposed
as a new problem, as a new theme, and even to supersede the
previous theme of his thinking which, then according to circumstances, our man will either "let out of his grip" entirely
or at least set aside temporarily.

It is not necessary to expand on the slight modifications
brought into the situation if the room entered is not the "home"
of the subject but a room with which he has not become familiar
so far. Nevertheless, even in such a case he has more or less well
defined expectations of what he may find in this *type* of room.
An object like that in the corner does not belong to the type of
things he may expect in this kind of room. Among all the other
more or less familiar or unproblematic things, this one stands
out by its unexpectedness. What might it be? It evokes his
curiosity, invites him to pay attention to it, to recognize or possibly identify it, to set him at ease as regards the other typicalities of his expectations. It becomes problematic to him and
therefore thematic.

*C. Topical Relevance and the Concept of Familiarity; Imposed
and Intrinsic Relevances*

This is the *first form* of relevance: namely, that by virtue of
which something is constituted as problematic in the midst of
the unstructuralized field of unproblematic familiarity—and
therewith the field into theme and horizon. We shall call this
kind *topical relevance*. It is worthwhile to note parenthetically
the fact that the Greek root of the term "problem" is equivalent
in its meaning to the Latin root of the term "object." The
original meaning of both is "that which is thrown before me."
As used in modern languages, the word "problem" has under-
gone a very significant change of meaning and thereby lost its
original connotations: to our modern scheme of expression in
general, not any object is problematical, but only one which is

dubious or questionable.[9] But to make an object a problem, to make it the theme or topic of our thought, means nothing else than to conceive it as a dubious and questionable one, to segregate it from the background of unquestionable and unquestioned familiarity which is simply taken for granted.

The term "familiarity" deserves a short comment.[10] It might be interpreted objectively, that is, as something inherent to the already experienced things we speak of as familiar to us. Indeed, certain psychologists speak of qualities of familiarity *(Bekanntheitsqualitäten)* which things have for the perceiving subject as a kind of "tertiary quality" bestowed upon them. Of course, there are degrees of such familiarity: previously perceived objects identified or recognized as the same, objects similar to or like those which are identifiable and recognizable, objects unfamiliar as regards their unique individuality but determinable as belonging to a familiar species, objects which are known to us merely as belonging to a familiar type, objects belonging to the category of tools or utensils, that is, serving as typical means for typical ends (in which case, only the means-ends relation is familiar as to its type), and so on. But familiarity also has its subjective meaning—which refers on the one hand to the habits of the subject in recognizing, identifying, and choosing actual experiences under the types at hand in his actual stock of knowledge. These habits in turn are not only the outcome of the object's personal history, the sedimentation of which they are, but also a function of his actual circumstances, the situational setting within which these habits have been formed—the ten *tropoi* of Aenesidemus claim to be a classification of circumstances. On the other hand, the subjective meaning of familiarity refers to, so to speak, the demarcation line which the subject draws between that segment of the world which needs and that which does not need further investigation.

In other words, familiarity in this subjective sense is a func-

9. Julián Marías' study is remarkably similar to this. See his *Reason and Life: The Introduction to Philosophy* (New Haven, Yale University Press, 1954), pp. 4–7.

10. See below, Ch. 3, Sec. B.

tion of the level of investigation determined by the actual interests of the subject as regards how far a particular problem at hand has to be analyzed—that is, the determination of the conditions under which the task of translating the unfamiliar into familiar terms is to be considered as solved. What was just now called the "actual interest" of the subject is in turn dependent on the circumstances and the situation within which the problems have arisen, and also upon the system of problems to which the specific one pertains. *But this "actual interest" is itself a form of relevance,* which must not be confused with the topical relevance now under discussion; it must be studied separately later on.[11] To be sure, there is a close connection between both forms of relevance, but actual interest presupposes the existence of a problem and is therefore founded upon the topical relevance which constitutes the problem itself.

These preliminary remarks have not yet disposed of the analysis of topical relevance. Thus far we have merely analyzed one case, although an important one, of the constitution of the theme within the undifferentiated field. *This case concerned the way in which an unfamiliar experience imposes itself upon us by its very unfamiliarity.* We do not make this experience thematical by a volitive act, and that is why we call this kind of relevance *imposed relevance.*

But unfamiliar experiences are not the only ones which are imposed on us as thematic. There are many other kinds of imposed topical relevances. For instance, the experience of shock, which as we have seen is characteristic of any shift of the attention of consciousness and thereby for the leap from one province of meaning to another, imposes new topical relevances; so, too, does any nonvolitional change in the level of our personality involved, especially any change of relative intimacy into relative anonymity. Moreover, any sudden change in the dimensions of time in which each of us lives simultaneously imposes other topical relevances. More generally, any interruption or modification which necessitates discontinuing the idealizations of "and so on" and "again and again," which

11. See below, Ch. 3, Sec. D.

are at the root of all our experience, create imposed topical relevances.[12] Finally, as will be shown later on, topical relevances are imposed by means of *social interaction* determined by the acts of our fellowmen or our own as individuals or social groups.

On the other hand, there is a class of topical relevances which is entirely different from that discussed thus far (that is, those which are imposed). We may voluntarily structure a field into thematic kernel and horizonal background, and we may even by means of such an act determine the field itself as well as its limits. Psychologists have frequently considered this kind of thematizing under the heading of *voluntary attention*. This class has two subdivisions: the first consists of the voluntary replacing of one theme of thought with another by gradually superimposing one on the other—that is, *by enlarging or deepening the prevailing theme.* The second refers to the *voluntary shifting of attention* from one topic to another when there is no connection between them. *In the first case the original theme has been retained,* and the changed thematic kernel remains related to what was thematic up to that point. To be sure, what was just now horizonal has become thematic, but not in the sense of a new theme. It remains connected with the former theme (which I still have in my grip), but it has been expanded in such a way that elements which were formerly horizonal and are now thematic have become intrinsic to the theme. *In the second case,* that of shifting to a completely heterogeneous theme, however, *the former theme has been abandoned.* It is no longer in my grip. It may be that it has been dropped for good (for example, if I have finished my job, or if I have forgotten this theme entirely), or I may turn away from it only temporarily with the intention of returning to it after an interruption and then pick it up again at some later time.

12. For the Husserlian notion of idealization, see Husserl, *Formale und transzendentale Logik,* Sec. 74; *Erfahrung und Urteil,* Secs. 51 (b), 58, 61. See also Schutz, *CP 1,* "Husserl's Importance for the Social Sciences," 140–49, esp. 146; and *CP 3,* "Phenomenology and the Foundations of the Social Sciences (Ideas, Volume *3,* by Edmund Husserl)," 40–50.

This latter modification refers to the voluntary pauses in our
activities, to the alternation of working hours and hours of
leisure, a problem highly important for the theory of planning
or projecting (as the unification of our interests and activities),
which will have to be discussed later on.[13] But as regards most
of the cases of voluntary change to a heterogeneous topic, closer
examination will show that the hidden motive for this sudden
shift of attention consists of *a leap from one reality dimension
to another,* or in putting into play another level of personality,
or in a change of the interplay of the dimensions of time in
which we live simultaneously. The counterpointal structure of
the stream of consciousness may change its character because
other strains of it receive a particular accent through such
shifting of attention and thereby obtain predominance. These
categories, however, have already been mentioned under the
group of imposed topical relevances. As can be seen, the
boundary between these two classes is by no means rigid; the
distinction is, as sociologists say, of an "ideal-typical nature"
—that is, that very rarely is each of these types found in purity,
notwithstanding the heuristic value of studying each of them
separately.[14]

We therefore restrict the following remarks concerning the
nonimposed topical relevances to what we previously called the
first subdivision—namely, the *voluntary superimposition of
one theme by another while retaining the first in one's grip.*
Through such superimposition, new topical relevances come
into play. New data hitherto within the horizonal field of the
first theme become drawn into the thematic kernel. The theme
is, of course, always a theme within a field; each theme always
has its specific horizon. Husserl[15] has pointed out that horizon
has a twofold meaning: outer and inner horizon. The *outer*

13. Schutz did not include this topic in the present study. See, however, *CP 1,* "Choosing Among Projects of Action," 67–98; and *CP 2,*
"Tiresias, or Our Knowledge of Future Events," 277–93.
14. See Schutz's analysis of ideal types in *PSW,* pp. 176–250, esp.
pp. 186–201; and *CP 1,* "Common-Sense and Scientific Interpretation
of Human Action," 34–47.
15. See above, Ch. 1, n. 8.

horizon is used to designate everything which occurs simultaneously with the theme in the actual field of consciousness. But as well it is used to designate everything that refers by means of retentions and recollections to the genesis of the theme in the past, and by means of protentions and anticipations to its future potentialities. Beyond this, the outer horizon refers to everything connected with this actual field as the outcome of passive syntheses such as similarity, likeness, dissimilarity, and so on—in short, all the connections which the common psychology textbook considers under the heading of *association by local or temporal contiguity or by similarity*. It is well known how Husserl has overcome the difficulties of the age-old concept of associationism by means of his theory of theme and horizon.

On the other hand, there is the *inner horizon*. Once the theme has been constituted, it becomes possible to enter more and more deeply (perhaps indefinitely) into its structure: first through describing as completely as possible its features and their uniqueness, and then by analyzing its elements and their interrelationships and functional structures determining the process of "sedimentation" of which it is the outcome, and eventually by reestablishing and reperforming the polythetic steps by which its meaning, grasped now by us in a single monothetic glance, has been constituted.[16] The theme (or if you will the problem) is therefore itself an unlimited field for further thematizations. *It is in this sense the abbreviation, the locus, of a practically infinite number of topical relevances which may be developed by further thematization of its intrinsic contents.* But this "subthematization" (accomplished by exploring the inner horizon of the theme or by actualizing the virtual topical

16. An example of something constituted polythetically and then grasped monothetically would be, say, counting the four corners of a square and then grasping the square itself as a whole (as "one" thing); or, to give another instance, judging step-by-step, "The sky is blue," and grasping the judgment itself (as when I say, "The judgment, 'The sky is blue,' is false"). See Schutz, *PSW*, pp. 74–78; Husserl, *Formale und transzendentale Logik*, pp. 104, 143, 147, 282–85; and Husserl, *Ideen 1*, Sec. 119.

relevances constituting its meaning) must not be conceived as a breaking down of the whole into its parts. Theme and intrinsic topical relevances are but two names of the same configuration. By entering into and explicating the inner horizons, by putting into play these hidden potential topical relevances—in a word, by subthematizing the theme—the latter remains constant as the determining factor of all such subthematization. It is in this sense what we shall call the *paramount theme,* and remains in grip as the home base or the system of reference of its entire content of topical relevances—which are topical precisely because they are intrinsic to the paramount theme.

Of course, in the preceding we have described merely one dimension of the inner horizon intrinsic to the paramount theme. Of equal importance is another dimension, although the term "inner horizon" seems to be less adequate to designate it. Once the paramount theme has been established as the home base, it is itself just a system of intrinsic topical relevances that is connected with other systems of topical relevances to a theme of a higher order in relation to which it is subordinate or a mere subthematization. But as such it contains in its meaning references to this theme of a higher order, and these references can be made explicit without leaving the home base of the paramount theme, and the *theme of a higher order* itself proves to be merely a set of topical relevances subordinate to a theme of a still higher order, and so on. (It is probably not necessary to defend these statements against a misunderstanding that the terms "theme of a higher order" or "subordinate theme" contain any reference to value judgments. What is in question is the relationship of foundedness [*Fundierung*], that is, the relationship whereby the "higher theme" is founded upon the "lower" one which is currently in view.)

Thus the inner horizon of a theme may be explored by means of voluntary acts explicating on the one hand the topical relevances leading to subthematization, and on the other hand referring to themes of a higher order, without losing in either case the paramount theme from which the investigations started as its home base for all of these topical relevances. This ex-

REFLECTIONS ON THE PROBLEM OF RELEVANCE   33

ploration of the intrinsic structure consists in either case of pulling horizonal material into the thematic kernel. Precisely the same is the case if we take into consideration not the inner but the outer horizon. In either case the paramount theme is maintained as the home base and all referential structures of the topical relevances involved derive their meaning from the intrinsic meaning of the maintained paramount theme. Nevertheless, at any time this superimposing of thematic data, this exploring of ever-new topical relevances, is due to the voluntary shifting of our ray of attention in order to make explicit the implicit topical relevances which are intrinsic to the paramount theme.

We shall therefore call this system the intrinsic topical relevances, as opposed to the imposed topical relevances already discussed. Whereas in the latter system the articulation of the field into theme and horizon is imposed by the emergence of some unfamiliar experience, by a shift of the accent of reality from one province to another, and so on, it is characteristic of the system of intrinsic topical relevances that we may or may not direct our attention to the indications implicit in the paramount theme—indications which have the form of inner or outer horizonal structurizations or forms of topical relevances —that is, we may or may not transform these horizonal surroundings into thematic data. *This is probably one element of the technique which Carneades called "periodeusis."* But before we can properly enter into the discussion of this subject, we must round off our present analysis of the topical relevances with a few remarks in order to prevent possible misunderstandings.

First, it is not our intention to restrict the distinction between imposed and intrinsic relevances just discussed to this system of topical relevances. Indeed we shall presently study other kinds of relevances, and each time must inquire whether their cross-classification into imposed and intrinsic holds good for the type under scrutiny.

Secondly, we should say a word about the concept of the *paramount theme as home base.* We have noted that the intrinsic topical relevances are accessible to further subthematization by voluntarily transforming horizonal into thematical material. Thus, the system of intrinsic relevances presupposes that some topical relevances have already constituted a theme, it being immaterial whether this first theme has been constituted by the imposed or intrinsic type; in other words, whether it emerged as a theme by reason of the so-called selective activities of the mind or whether it has been passively received is irrelevant. It would be meaningless to search for a first theme (first chronologically) of our thinking since *there is no consciousness conceivable without structurization into theme and horizon.* It was, therefore, a merely pedagogical but entirely unrealistic assumption when we spoke in some places in the preceding pages of an "unarticulated" field of consciousness which by experiencing topical relevances may be structured into thematic kernel and horizonal material. Thematic structure, in other words, is essential to consciousness; that is, *there is always a theme within the field of consciousness,* and when we spoke of the constitution of a thematic kernel by means of imposed topical relevances, we merely meant that such an event was the motive for dropping what was previously thematic in favor of a new theme.

Third, it must be pointed out that *by the establishment of the paramount theme as home base both the direction of the intrinsic relevances leading into the horizon and the limit up to which they must be followed are to a certain extent already constituted.* To be sure, a voluntary act is needed to perform this translation of horizonal material into topical terms, but this freedom is limited. Concerning the direction to be followed, it should be stated that the system of intrinsic relevances is not to be conceived as homogeneous. It has its profile. Some of the relevances stand out over the others. It is a system of isohypses more comparable to the reproduction of a mountain chain in relief than on the usual map. This problem will have to be studied later on.[17]

Concerning the point up to which the intrinsic relevances

17. See below, Ch. 3, Sec. F.

should be followed, we have here a situation quite similar to that of the subjective meaning of familiarity. *It is the set of "actual interests," which itself depends upon the autobiographical and situational circumstances of the individual that limit what is commonly called the level of investigation* (that is, the borderline up to which a segment of the world has to be put into question), whereas everything beyond this borderline remains unquestioned (although not unquestionable and, so long as it is not questioned, simply taken for granted). This, too, will be investigated later on.[18]

Fourth, our entire description of the situation may create the erroneous impression that, except for the hierarchical structure of subthemes, paramount themes, themes of a higher order, each theme is given at a certain moment to the mind in isolation and could be handled as such. This is by no means the case. *The theme is always not only within a field but also connected to other themes which together form a system.* There is no such thing as an isolated problem but rather systems of problems, each interrelated with the other; but in order to study this highly complex situation we must do a good deal of preparatory analysis. We will, however, approach one part of the complexities involved if we now continue our analysis of Carneades' example: the case, that is, of two competing interpretations of the same theme.

D. The Interpretative Relevance

Thus far we have followed the man in this example merely up to the point where he discovers an unfamiliar object within an otherwise familiar, or at least typically familiar, anticipated surrounding. This something in the corner has become of topical relevance to him. It appeals to his curiosity, attracts his attention. The thing as such—or perhaps better, *the thing as it appears to him* in its surroundings, the thing as *phenomenon* perceived with all its noematico-noetical implications—is now thematically given to him for interpretation. What might it be?

18. See below, Ch. 3, Sec. B.

The solution to this question is the new task the man must perform in order *to grasp the meaning of what is now within the
thematic kernel of his conceptual*[19] *field.* He must interpret it;
and that means that he has to subsume it, as to its typicality,
under the various typical prior experiences which constitute
his actual stock of knowledge at hand. *But not everything
within the latter is used as a scheme of interpretation.* His
knowledge of the fact that all human beings are mortal, that
the sun rises every day in the east, that the constitution of others
shows such-and-such a feature, is entirely unconnected with the
interpretation of this particular visual object before him now.

However, by means of what Husserl calls the *passive synthesis of recognition,* he superimposes the actual perception of
a corporeal object of such-and-such shape, such-and-such extension, such-and-such color with the recollection of previous
perceptions of corporeal objects having typically similar, like,
or same shape, extension, color, and so on. Within the context
of his previous experiences (of any kind) as preserved by memory and arranged by previous interpretations into his stock of
knowledge actually at hand, there are many which have nothing
to do with the interpretation of the object before him, which
are entirely *irrelevant* for interpreting this new object. On the
other hand, there are a few coherent types of previous experiences with which the present object might be compared—that
is, interrelated by sameness, likeness, similarity, and so on.
We may call the latter *relevant* elements for his interpreting
of the new set of perceptions; but it is perfectly obvious that
this kind of relevance is quite different from that studied this far
and which we have called the topical relevances. We therefore
suggest that this new category be termed the *interpretative
relevances.*

This kind of relevance reveals, however, *a curious double
function. Not only is it interpretatively relevant that part of our
stock of knowledge at hand has "something to do" with the*

19. Although Schutz uses "conceptual" here, it would seem from the
context that "perceptual" would be more accurate. What is at issue is
the interpretation of a visually perceived object and its surroundings.

thematic object now given to our interpretation; but, uno actu, *certain particular moments of the object perceived obtain the character of major or minor interpretative relevance for the task of recognizing and interpreting the actually experienced segment of the world.*

Returning to our example, it may be sufficient to identify a pile of rope as such according to its Gestalt (extension, shape, color, etc.) without asking what the material or the weight of this rope may be. Even the color might prove to be irrelevant. Assuming that I have previous experiences of piles of brown and black rope, I may still recognize the present object (which has, say, a gray color) as a "pile of rope" although I have never seen a pile of gray rope before. In such a case, it would be "like" rope I have previously experienced, *but* gray. Moreover, I may have a very good idea of rope but not of rope placed in piles; and, on the other hand, of piles of things but not consisting of rope; and nevertheless ascertain this something before me now as a pile of rope—"rope," incidentally arranged in the shape of a pile; a pile incidentally formed by rope; this rope having in addition and in the present situation, perfectly incidentally, a gray color. It is the whole setting—locally, temporally, autobiographically, and, as we will later see, that in which the object to be interpreted appears—which will determine, on the one hand, the moments of this object (its perceptual phenomena) and, on the other, the elements of my stock of knowledge at hand which are interpretatively relevant with respect to one another. This complexity should become clearer as we proceed with our analysis.

Let us assume that our man has in one way or another succeeded in identifying the rope before him as possibly ($\pi\iota\theta\alpha\nu\acute{o}\nu$) being a pile of rope. To borrow a form of description of this sort of impression from William James we might say that he perceives "object-in-room-corner-possibly-being-gray-rope-pile."[20] The interpretative relevances adherent to the moments

20. Cf. James, *Principles of Psychology, 1,* 240–45; also Schutz, *CP 3,* "William James' Concept of the Stream of Thought Phenomenologically Interpreted," 1–14.

of shape, extension, Gestalt, color, and so on, entered into play, and it is these that made possible the recognition of this object as belonging to the previously experienced type "rope pile"—*possible but not yet probable*. The degree of likelihood bestowed on this first interpretative guess will depend very much on the *whole situation* in which this guess is made.

Let us now assume that an object like the one in question is perceived on board a vessel. To all my experiences of the type "vessel" belongs the expectation that piles of rope can and probably will be found. The familiarity of this expectation may reach such a high degree that no thematic relevance will be imposed upon an observer of such an object. It may remain in the background of the "natural," that is the unquestioned, surroundings. Correspondingly the perception of the object may never lose its horizonal quality; it may never become thematized unless, for instance, a question by a child ("What is this thing in the dark corner?") may bring into play the topical relevances upon which the interpretational diagnosis follows: "This is a pile of rope." Although there will always be the possibility that closer examination—that is both with respect to the change of the perception and to the reinterpretation of these changes—might reveal that the object in question is not a pile of rope but a snake, the first guess ("This is a pile of rope") has for the speaker a high degree of probability. Or, in other words, there is an excellent chance that later verification will prove his statement to be true. He therefore gives his "assent" to the first interpretative guess and will continue to behave as if this verification had already occurred. He will act in this way until some new element of topical relevance (for instance, the shifting of the thematic field into the inner or outer horizon: "Let us have a better look at it") *or* a newly emergent moment of interpretative revelance refutes or contradicts his first diagnosis. Then the meaning of his first guess and the whole system of interpretative relevances adhering to it will lose their coherence and compatibility. They will, to use a Husserlian term, "explode," become annihilated, stricken out as void. But as long as such counterproof does not occur, the validity of the first guess will be simply taken for granted: is it not quite plausible to encounter a pile of rope on board a vessel?

Let us now vary the example slightly[21] and suppose that the object in question is not observed on board a vessel but rather in the corner of a friend's room, who as I know is a sailor. The likelihood (the "subjective chance") that my first interpretation will prove to be correct is considerably diminished: is it customary, can it plausibly be expected, that one would find a pile of rope inside a house? Of course, the presence of such an object in a sailor's house might not be unusual; at least, no interpretative relevances originating in the total setting indicate the contrary. To be sure, even if we suppose that I have never seen rope of such a color and also that the shape of a pile is not the usual form in which I have observed rope before, nevertheless my first guess ("This is a pile of rope") is quite plausible in the context of my sailor-friend's house, it has its own weight, and nothing contradicts for the time being its implicated interpretative relevances. My doubting of this interpretation will begin if the supposed pile of rope starts to "behave" otherwise than topically expected: for example, the object starts to move. Then I may ask: "Was my first guess correct? Could not the interpretative relevances of shape, color, etc., involved also remain valid if this thing were something else, perhaps a snake?"

But suppose I return to my own home. Being neither a sailor nor a fisherman, and not having the habit of having anything to do with rope, should I find in a badly illuminated corner of my home a strange object which has not been there before and the presence of which does not comply with any of my expectations concerning what I usually find in this room, I regard this object without any preconceived scheme concerning its interpretational relevances. If there are, as it is wisely assumed in Carneades' example, additional situational elements (for ex-

21. Schutz's method here is that of "free variation": to vary systematically in order to determine which characteristics stand out as invariant (i.e. essential) to the thing in question. Cf. Husserl, *Ideen 1,* Sec. 70.

ample, it is wintertime, I am pusillanimous), I may immediately
draw the conclusion from the same interpretationally relevant
moments pertaining to the object, "This is a snake." Certainly
this would have equal weight with the guess that it is a pile of
rope. The presence of either snake or rope does not fulfill any
prior expectations; its shape, color, Gestalt are intrinsically
relevant to both: the typical pile of rope and the typical coiled
snake as I find these types already formed within my stock of
knowledge at hand. Either of these first guesses would be
equally possible (πιθανόν) and neither would have "more
weight" than the other. My doubt concerning the correctness of
the interpretation (it being immaterial which of the two assumed guesses was chronologically prior) begins immediately,
and I must at least suspend my "assent" until I am able to establish additional interpretative relevances.

It seems to me that this situation corresponds exactly to that
designated by Carneades as περίσπαστος. Two interpretations
of the same thematic object are equally possible, one having
equal weight with the other while yet being incompatible with
it. How is that so? The interpretative relevances are not sufficiently complete to make an unequivocal determination possible. The uncertainty will only increase if, for instance, I suppose that I have never seen rope formed in piles, or a rope of
gray color, or snakes of such a color coiled in such a manner.
Both interpretations will lead to the assumption of the presence
of a strange object in my room—it being as implausible that
during my absence someone has placed a pile of rope in that
corner as that a snake has chosen this place for its hibernation.
It is, moreover, important for me to make a decision.[22] I can
do so merely by completing the interpretative relevances; but in
order to do this, I must compare typical moments of the percepts with typical moments of my previous experiences of
other typical rope piles or typical snakes. For example: the object does not move, and this seems to enhance the possibility
that it is lifeless; but hibernating snakes do not move either.

22. Schutz notes that this statement "will have to be analyzed presently"

The enhancement of the weight of the first hypothesis is counterbalanced by the increased weight of the second one. In the language of Carneades, I do not succeed in establishing an "unbent" representation since each interpretatively relevant moment remains ambiguous ($\pi\epsilon\rho\acute{\iota}\sigma\pi\alpha\sigma\tau\sigma$), and even if I continue my periodeusis, that is, the completion of the interpretative relevances of the thematic material, I do not arrive at a sufficient completeness—sufficient for assenting to one of the two possible interpretations as more plausible than the other. It is at this moment that I decide to make the experiment with the stick, hoping to determine how the object to be interpreted will react and to gain new interpretatively relevant material from the observation of its immediately future behavior.

Before analyzing this new phase, however, we must complete our analysis of interpretative relevances. Many authors, including Husserl, seem inclined to conceive the hesitation between doubtful interpretations as an oscillating between two themes (or at least they leave this point in abeyance). Contrary to this, we submit that only one theme prevails throughout the whole process as paramount. What is thematic is always the percept of this same strange object in the corner of my room— an object of such-and-such a shape, color, extension, and so on. At least we may say, the noema of this percept remains unchanged despite all possible noetical variations.[23] But on the other hand, it is true that in order to collect new interpretatively relevant moments intrinsic to the same thematic object, I must shift my attentional focus in such a way that data which were horizonal are drawn into the thematic kernel—a procedure which has already been described. *In performing the periodeusis, I must "examine" more carefully the object and its moments, which thus enter into its thematic inner horizon.* Taking into account its situational determination (strangeness with re-

23. The terms "noema" and "noesis" are used by Schutz, following Husserl, to designate, respectively, the "object-*as*-experienced" (perceived, remembered, valued, judged, or whatever) and the "experiencing-of-the-object." Cf., e.g., *Ideen 1*, Secs. 87–96; and Gurwitsch, *The Field of Consciousness*, Chs. 2 and 3.

spect to the local surroundings, and so on), I must expand the
thematical kernel into its outer horizon as well. Nevertheless, in
spite of all these variations, the percept of this same object
remains my home base, my paramount theme which is never
out of grip. It is even, it would seem, only a terminological
question whether we should speak of subthematization in such
cases.

Are interpretative relevances to be qualified as imposed or as
intrinsic? In the various phases just described, they can be
either. The first guess, originating in the passive synthesis of
recognition, certainly lacks any volitional character. Automatically, so to speak (that is, by means of passive synthesis),
the object is perceived as being "similar," "like," "of the type
as," this and that typically already experienced object. It is, as
was already pointed out, not merely perceived as "something,"
or "something-in-room-corner," or even "corporeal-object-in-
room-corner"; rather, from the outset it is perceived as either
"object-in-room-corner-possibly-being-gray-rope-pile" or as
"object-in-room-corner-possibly-being-snake." But as soon as
I am aware, this first interpretation is moot ($\pi\epsilon\rho\acute{\iota}\sigma\pi\alpha\sigma\tau\sigma s$), precisely because the interpretative relevances founding this first
guess are not unequivocally determinable—they may hold good
for another interpretation which is incompatible with the first
one. In other words, as soon as problematic possibilities, alternatives in the strict sense, have been established as equally
plausible interpretations of the same "state-of-affairs," or as
soon as the periodeutical process starts, the additional interpretative relevances will be obtained by a volitional turning to
the intrinsic moments of the paramount theme. Consequently,
the interpretative relevances of my first guess are experienced
as imposed; the examination of the plausibility of such interpretation, the possible assent, doubt, putting into question the
ascertainment of its "weight," justification, or annihilation,
and the like, originate in volitional activities. It is the latter
which transform the imposed relevant moments of the perceptual theme into intrinsic interpretative relevances.

This presentation of the process of interpretation might lead to the misunderstanding that interpreting belongs to the predicative sphere and occurs in a chain of logical steps passing from premises to conclusions. This is by no means necessarily so. In *Erfahrung und Urteil,* Husserl has clearly shown that what we call *interpretation and interpretative relevances originate within the prepredicative sphere* and are as such not inferential.[24] Indeed, certain categories of logical judgments, as well as certain forms of syllogism, are founded on these prepredicative experiences. This circumstance, of course, does not imply that in the supervening procedure of establishing intrinsic interpretative relevances, purely inferential procedures may not be used.

In any case, what has been noted as regards topical relevances is true as well for the interpretational type: there are no such things as isolated relevances. Whatever their type, they are always interconnected and grouped together in systems, just as are the various systems of relevances within any one category—as, for instance, the two studied thus far. The interpretatively relevant moment of both—the experience to be interpreted and the scheme of interpretation (i.e. the applicable previous experiences as found in our stock of knowledge at hand)—are integrated into systems, and these systems, at least as to their type, as well as the typical ways in which they are applied, are within the stock of what we have already experienced. Such already acquired experience has its genetic and autobiographically determined history and is itself the sediment of habitually acquired practice. Not only the topical but also the interpretative relevances (and the acts of interpreting, assenting, questioning, doubting, deciding, and so forth) are all situationally conditioned. We have to *learn* what is interpretatively relevant; we must learn in the course of our actual experiences how to recognize interpretatively relevant moments or aspects of objects already experienced as typical. Further-

24. Cf. *Erfahrung und Urteil,* Secs. 82 and 83, and also the Introduction and Part I.

---

more, we have to learn how to "weigh" the outcome of our interpretations, how to determine the impact of circumstantial modifications inherent in the situation in which such interpreting occurs, how to complete and to coordinate the interpretatively relevant material, and so on. The adult, wide-awake man will not experience what he sees in the dark corner merely as "something," but at least as a corporeal object having extension, color, shape, and the like. But even more, although he may well question whether the corporeal object before him is a pile of rope or a snake, or a piece of cloth, he will never interpret it as, say, a table, or a dog—in spite of the fact that these objects may also be colored gray. *The system of interpretative relevances is founded,* in short, *upon the principle of compatibility* —or, as Leibniz would call it, of compossibility—*of all of its coexistent moments.* And for this very reason the volitional acts which supervene in establishing additional intrinsic interpretative relevances are limited in scope (not every one is freely available), precisely as are the acts establishing intrinsic topical relevances.

To review the discussion, in studying the intrinsic topical relevances we have examined the question concerning how far the intrinsic relevances have to be followed. We noted that the level of investigation beyond which everything seems to be unquestionably granted and up to which it must be put in question depends upon what we called our "actual interest." This interest is itself, we said, a function of the situational circumstances. We may now raise the question whether a similar criterion can be found with respect to the limits up to which intrinsic interpretative relevances have to be developed. Doubtless, this point is reached to the extent that we can "assent" to our interpretation; but this assent may itself have different degrees of certitude, as Carneades developed in his theory of the πιθανόν: plausibility, probability, likelihood, possibility. It is indeed the degree of certainty which is defined by our "actual interest" (the meaning of which will have to be determined; but for the moment this may be left open). If, as in our example, I hesitate to interpret the object in the corner of my room as a pile of rope or as a serpent, my actual interest requires a much higher degree of certainty than if I am in doubt whether it is a pile of rope or a pile of clothes.

Beyond this, the variations of the example—i.e. considering the same object on board a vessel, in the house of a sailor, in my own home—have clearly shown to what extent the degree of certainty which will satisfy me depends upon the situational circumstances which, in turn, define my actual interest. On the other hand, it is the degree of plausibility thus established which determines the number and weight of interpretative relevances considered as sufficient to warrant the success of my interpretation. (This fact proves the validity, but also shows the limits, of the operationalistic argument which Dewey and his followers have unilaterally established as the foundation of their epistemological theory.) My interpretation, however, remains tentative, subject to verification or falsification by supervening interpretatively relevant material.

E. The Motivational Relevance; in-order-to and because Motives

We may now return to another phase of Carneades' example. The man, unable to come to an interpretative decision based upon the interpretatively relevant material at hand, takes his stick and hits the object. We have already stated that he does this because the diagnosis of the nature of this object is *important* to him. Importance as used here is clearly related to the notion of relevance. But this kind of relevance is neither topical nor interpretational. It does not refer to the articulation of his field of consciousness into theme or horizon because this field and its articulations have remained unchanged. Nor does it refer to the interpretatively relevant material at hand, because this material, incomplete and ambiguous as it is, did not lead to a satisfactory diagnosis. What could have been disclosed is merely an "either-or": "the object is either a pile of rope or a snake." Such an either-or statement might be considered as having quite satisfactory plausibility in many other cases; having arrived at it, our curiosity or "interest" in this problem and its interpretation might simply be exhausted. Why, then, not stop here and turn away toward more gratifying tasks?

But in our example this does not happen. The decision concerning which alternative is to be followed is of vital importance for planning the man's future behavior. There is certainly no reason for not sleeping in a room which contains a harmless pile of rope, or for removing this object from the room. But there is an obvious danger for either of these should the object turn out to be a snake. Hence, the correct (or, at least, the satisfactory) interpretative choice will clearly determine the man's future conduct. He will act differently according to which he chooses; that is, he will in either case project different goals to be realized by means of his actions, and accordingly he will effect different means for bringing about the projected state of affairs. He will in short base his *decision concerning how to act on the interpretative decision,* and thus the latter will determine the former. The importance of interpreting correctly (and this means here to a satisfactorily plausible degree) consists in the fact that not only the means to be chosen but even the ends to be attained will depend upon such a diagnosis. The satisfactorily plausible degree of interpretation opens a relatively high subjective chance of meeting the situation efficiently by appropriate countermeasures—or at least it shows the risk of any move even if no appropriate (i.e. efficient) countermeasures can be taken. In either case, the outcome of the periodeusis will be relevant for the man's future action. We shall call this type of relevance the *motivational relevances*.

But the importance of the interpretative decision for the planning of future conduct is not the only motivational relevance involved in the present example. In order to avoid danger in entering my room by removing the object, I have to come to an interpretational decision. To come to such a decision, I must obtain additional interpretatively relevant material. And in order for me to find such material, I have to create different observational conditions, and then to see whether they will furnish new indications. Changing the observational conditions, furthermore, requires that I act on the object in such a way that its expected reaction might be of interpretative relevance. In order to provoke a reaction by a live organism, I must hit it (since I know, by means of my previous experience, that such objects react quite differently than do lifeless ones if they are hit). In order to hit it without danger to myself, I have to make use of another object, such as a stick. In order to do this, I have to grasp the stick, swing my arm, and so on.

Each of the preceding sentences—which either could or does begin with an "in order to"—indicates motivational relevances, such that what has to be done is motivated by that for which it is to be done, the latter being motivationally relevant for the former. It is a chain of interrelated motivational relevances which leads to the decision concerning how I must act.

But that is a rather awkward and confusing way to express the highly complicated correlation between the motivating and the motivated. On the one hand we said that the interpretational decision is motivationally relevant for the course of action to be adopted; on the other, that the goal of such action (to avoid danger) motivates in turn the process of obtaining additional interpretative material. How are these two statements related? Which of them, the goal of action or the successful interpretation, motivates the other?

The ambiguity between motivating and motivated experiences is not merely a terminological one. The concept of motivational relevance which we have advanced here only indicates the correlation of motivating and motivated experiences, without making any assertion concerning what motivates and what is motivated. When we analyzed the structure of interpretative relevances, we observed a similar situation. The selection and correlation of the interpretatively relevant moments of actual experiences with those of similar previous experiences is established *uno actu*. As soon as a moment m, observed on the actually perceived object, strikes me as being relevant, I have to correlate it with previously experienced objects showing the same moment m, even if the set of moments n, o, p on the observed object cannot be correlated to the previously experienced object (which, instead of m, n, o, p, shows the moments m, r, s, t). The moment m is then inter-

48 ALFRED SCHUTZ

pretationally relevant for both. Precisely the same holds for
the category of motivational relevance. To learn that one step
is "important" for another establishes the motivational relevance of both with respect to one another, without implying
anything as regards which of them is chronologically prior, nor
which is the efficient cause of the other. More generally, we
may say that the category of relevance—topical, interpretational, motivational—establishes merely a correlation between
two terms having reciprocal import as regards one another.

But as this seems merely to beg the question, closer analysis
of the concept of motive is necessary.[25] The dictionary defines
motive as any idea, need, etc. that impels to action. But it can be
seen immediately that this definition covers two entirely different situations, which we shall have to consider separately.

On the one hand, there is the idea of the state of affairs to be
brought about by the action which impels us to act. This future
state of affairs, the projected goal to be attained by our subsequent acting, is phantasized by us before we start our action.
It is the "idea" which "impels" us to act, the motive of our
going ahead; that is, we act *in order to* bring about the state of
affairs. We call this kind of motive the "in-order-to" motive of
our acting; in the chain of sentences discussed above, it was
this type of motive we had in mind. The state of affairs to be
brought about, the motive which is of paramount relevance for
all succeeding steps, is the removal of the object while keeping
out of danger. In order to do so, I must find out whether it is a
snake; in order to find this out, I must hit it with a stick, etc., etc.

If I place myself at the moment *before* I begin to act, merely
projecting the state of affairs to be brought about and the single

25. For Schutz's detailed analysis of in-order-to and because motives,
see *PSW*, pp. 86–96. Briefly, the first type concerns acts "projected in the
future perfect tense and in terms of which the action receives its orientation . . . [that is] a project within which the completed act is pictured
as something to be brought to fulfillment by my action." (pp. 88–89) The
second concerns acts in which "both the motivating and the motivated
lived experiences have the temporal character of pastness . . . and we
can therefore designate our intentional reference to it as *thinking in
the pluperfect tense*" (p. 93).

steps relevant for actualizing this goal, I may say that the phantasied state of affairs aimed at motivates the single steps to be taken for its actualization. If, however, I place myself at a moment *after my action has already begun,* I may express exactly the same situation by means of a chain of "because" sentences. Reaching for my stick, for example, I might answer my friend's query, "What are you doing here?" as follows: "I need this stick because I want to hit this object. I want to do this because I want to find out whether it is a snake. I want to do this because I want to be sure that I can remove this object without danger." It is clear that this is a merely linguistically different way of expressing the same thing. The first chain of in-order-to sentences is logically equivalent to the second chain of because sentences, for in both the state of affairs to be brought about, the paramount project, motivates the single steps to be taken. In other words, the paramount project is motivationally relevant for the projecting of the single steps; the single steps to be performed are, however, "causally relevant" for bringing about the desired result.

But this "causal relevance," as will be shown later on (when we discuss the problem of "adequate causality"),[26] is nothing but the objective corollary to what is subjectively experienced as "motivationally relevant." With respect to human action, in short, *any statement of causal relevancy can be easily translated into terms of motivational relevance and the adherent systems of interpretational relevance.*[27] Within the frame of our present study of subjective motives of action, therefore, there is no special reason for augmenting the catalogue of the various kinds of relevance by introducing a special category of causal relevance; we may thus reserve this term for use in another context.

26. Not included in the present study; but see *PSW,* pp. 229–32.
27. Schutz noted parenthetically here that "The highly complicated interrelationship between systems of motivational, interpretative, and topical relevance will be discussed presently." Cf. below, Ch. 3, esp. Sec. F. In *PSW,* Schutz was already very close to the conception of relevance developed in the present study; Cf. esp. pp. 85–86.

The because sentences discussed thus far have proved to be
merely another form of in-order-to sentences, and all such sentences will be called *spurious* because sentences. But there are
because statements which cannot be so translated, and analysis
of this type leads us to the second sense of the ambiguous term
"motive"—namely, the *genuine because motive*.

I want to investigate the object in question *because* I fear that
it is a snake. My fearing snakes is a genuine because motive of
my project of reaching a decision. Other people may call me
pusillanimous, but this is not experienced by me as such. It is
the objective term for my subjective, biographically determined
situation of fearing snakes, and this fear is what impels me to
project the removal of the object without endangering myself.
This is a genuine because motive, for my fear is motivationally
relevant for phantasying the paramount project which in turn
becomes (in the way of in-order-to) motivationally relevant
for each single step to be taken in order to actualize the projected state of affairs.

*Whereas the in-order-to relevances motivationally emanate
from the already established paramount project, the because
relevances deal with the motivation for the establishment of the
paramount project itself.* It would be senseless to say that I
fear snakes in order to establish the paramount project of removing the presumptively dangerous object. My fear of snakes
is motivationally relevant for considering this object as dangerous, provided it is a snake, and for projecting its removal
with a maximum of safety. Thus, my fear of snakes is also
mediately motivationally relevant for the limits up to which
I have to follow the intrinsic interpretational relevances in
order to be satisfied with the plausibility-degree of the outcome
of this interpretation. But not only is this the case, for my
fear of snakes might be motivationally relevant for the establishment of the either-or alternative, that of "problematic possibility": "this is either a pile of rope or a snake," instead of:
"this is either a pile of rope or a pile of clothes." Finally, my
fear might even be motivationally relevant for the system of
topical relevances for focusing this and no other object in the

dark corner as worth my attention. But on the other hand, my fear of snakes has its autobiographical history as well, referring to many series of previously experienced relevances—topical, interpretational, and motivational ones which now "subconsciously" stir the tension of my consciousness and determine the intimacy of the level of personality involved. The technique of psychoanalysts, considered briefly in a previous section of this study, is based upon this interrelationship between the various types of relevances. Conversely, the system of interpretational relevances, especially as regards its increase in plausibility, may be motivationally relevant for the building up of new intrinsic topically relevant systems. Other possible combinations of interrelationships between the three systems of relevances will be dealt with in the following chapter.

We must still examine, although only briefly, whether the motivational relevances reveal the same features as the topical and interpretational ones. As we have seen, there are no isolated motivational relevances; they appear in the form of systems, of "chains" interconnected with one another. We introduced the term "paramount project" to delineate the point beyond which the actor's actual interest no longer requires that he pursue this chain of motivational interconnectedness. It is he and not the observer of his action who is alone able to draw this line—which corresponds to what has been previously called the level of investigation. As regards projecting and acting, we are merely interested in the motivational relevances of the in-order-to type as they emanate from the situation at hand—i.e. the situation which we, the actors, have to "define" (as sociologists call it).[28] But we may, and indeed always can, shift the focus of our interest in such a way that we

28. Cf. W. I. Thomas' collected papers, *Social Behavior and Personality, Contributions of W. I. Thomas to Theory and Social Research,* ed. Edmund H. Volkart (New York, Social Science Research Council, 1951), esp. pp. 14, 80 ff.; and his book, *The Child in America: Behavior Problems and Programs* (New York, Alfred A. Knopf, 1927), p. 572. Schutz treats the issues esp. in *CP 1,* "Common-Sense and Scientific Interpretation of Human Action," 9–10; and "Concept and Theory Formation in the Social Sciences," 54–55.

draw new motivationally relevant material into the topically relevant focus. A special situation arises here, however: living in our action we have different interest in its motivationally relevant moments than when we merely project such an action, or when we look back at an action already performed in respect of its outcome or the single steps by which it was actualized and the project which preceded it. In each of these instances, other chains of elements will prove to be motivationally relevant. The reason for this is that our actual interest accompanying each of these attitudes is different. The following chapter will attempt to clarify this.

Motivational relevances may be therefore imposed or intrinsic. We will at a later point be especially interested in the socially imposed motivational relevances. But even as regards the isolated individual's experiences, merely the choice of the paramount project (or what the actor considers at the actual moment as his paramount project) is intrinsically motivationally relevant. It alone originates in a volitional act of his own. Once constituted, all motivational relevances deriving from the paramount project are experienced as being imposed. There is a special problem involved relating to the type of action called rational acts. In consists in a transformation of imposed relevances into intrinsic ones and in a διέξοδος as complete as possible preceding the establishment of the paramount project.[29]

29. This chapter concludes with the note that it was originally written in Lake Placid, September 2, 1947.

As we have seen, the three categories of relevance studied thus
far are interconnected with one another in many respects. The
analysis of these refers us to what we have called our stock of
knowledge at hand prevailing at any particular autobiographical moment. The latter term, however, is but another heading
for a set of rather complex problems which will have to be
analyzed carefully. Our remarks relating to the interconnectedness of the various systems of relevance are, therefore, preliminary and restricted to the purpose of making a new set of
problems visible.

A. The Habitual Possessions of Knowledge

We return to the last part of the example we have been using.
We found that my fear of snakes was motivationally relevant
both for my wish to investigate and determine the strange object
in the corner of my room, and to the set of in-order-to motives
guiding the actions by means of which a decision resolving my
doubt might be made. But what does it mean that my fear of
snakes becomes the because motive of my actual experiences?
Before having entered the room, even before having grasped the
idea that the object in the corner might be a snake, I did not
think of snakes or my fear of them at all. My fear was up to then
perfectly irrelevant. It is nevertheless true that I am what char-
acterologists call pusillanimous. I fear a great many things,

1. This chapter had the following note attached: "Estes Park, 27
VII 1951 (replacing ms August, 1950)."

among them snakes especially. This is not continuously present in my consciousness, nor do I suffer the neurosis of being constantly on the lookout for snakes. But my fear of them is always potentially present, so to speak in a neutral manner, but ready to be actualized at any moment when circumstances are such that the presence of snakes becomes plausible. My fear is in this sense a *habitual possession;* it is *a potential set of typical expectations to be actualized under typical circumstances leading to typical reactions* or (in our terminology) *to the building up of a paramount project of possible action involving the whole chain of in-order-to motives relating to the carrying out of the paramount project as, if, and when needed.* Under certain circumstances I am prepared to translate this paramount project into reality in the same manner in which the chiefs of staff of an army during peacetime are ready immediately to carry out well-prepared strategical plans should an enemy attack the country in a particular way. Psychologists and social scientists might be inclined to call this my habitual possession of certain motives, latent for the time being but always ready to be actualized, an "attitude." My attitude toward snakes, it might be said, is fear. Yet, being admittedly pusillanimous, I fear not only snakes but many other things—such as spirits, murderers, diseases, and the like. Is not my pusillanimity generally my attitude to the world, and my fearing snakes just a particular case of it?

I do not know whether I can explain why I became pusillanimous, and under ordinary circumstances the fact that I am so is not topically relevant to me. Should the latter happen, I would probably have to turn to a psychiatrist or psychoanalyst to overcome this attitude. But considering my fear of snakes, I am sure that this "habitual possession" has its history and is determined by autobiographical circumstances. Suppose, for instance, that as a child I had an adventure with a snake and was told how dangerous some of these creatures can be. At the time, the typical shape, color, behavior of a snake, up until then not only irrelevant but even unknown to me, became topically relevant. I learned to become aware of the existence of a new problem, and I also learned typical ways of solving it (e.g. avoiding them, running away, striking with a stick, etc.). Once solved, the problem lost its topical interest for me. Being no longer thematic, I turned to other tasks, the experience was even dismissed from my field of consciousness. It was, if not forgotten, at least no longer in view. Nevertheless, this adventure with a particular snake led to the acquisition of a particular knowledge of the typical appearance of snakes, their behavior, their danger, and typical ways to avoid such dangers. It will depend upon my instruction and experience whether this knowledge has the form, "All snakes are dangerous and must be avoided," or "Some snakes are dangerous and I must ascertain which species are dangerous and then avoid them," or "Under certain circumstances some snakes may become dangerous and I have to avoid meeting those which are dangerous under such circumstances." The knowledge I thus acquire will also include typical, more or less detailed recipes telling me how to avoid such dangers, and typical emotions which will accompany from now on my looking at or thinking about snakes—namely, fear.

In more general terms, *my motivational relevances are sedimentations of previous experiences, once topically or interpretationally relevant* ("dangerous snakes have these and those characteristics") *to me, which led to a permanent habitual possession of knowledge*—remaining dormant as long as the former topical relevances do not recur, but which become actualized if the "same" situation or a typically similar one ("the same situation but modified," "a like situation," "a similar situation," etc.) recurs. By means of this very knowledge I think that I am *familiar* with what a snake looks like and how it typically behaves. If, in the future, I encounter (say, in another country and under other circumstances) a reptile of a kind which "I have never seen before"—that is, which differs in color, size, etc., from all snakes I have ever seen—I will nevertheless recognize it as "a snake and possibly dangerous," and because I fear snakes, this possibly harmless reptile and its properties will become topically relevant to me. My habitual possession of previously acquired knowledge will enable me to recognize the object as a snake and to recognize the possible danger.

B. Familiarity and Strangeness; Types and Typicality; Things Taken For Granted

This example is instructive as well because it helps to clarify the concepts of *familiarity* and *strangeness*.[2] I am familiar with snakes but merely with what I believe to be typical characteristics of snakes, including their typical behavior. That does not mean that I am familiar with all particular snakes or even with this particular species of snake, a specimen of which I now encounter. Nevertheless, I ascertain this reptile as being a snake and not, say, a lizard. On the other hand, to meet this particular species of snake, and this individual snake, is to me a new experience. A new experience is not necessarily a novel one. It may be new but still, as our example has shown, familiar as to its type.

But although being familiar as to its type, it is strange insofar as it is *atypical* in its uniqueness and particularity. My Irish setter Fido has the typical traits of all dogs and the particular traits of the species Irish setter. In addition, Fido has certain characteristics in his appearance and behavior which are exclusively his own and which permit me to recognize him as "my Fido" over against all other Irish setters, dogs, mammals, animals, objects in general—the typicality of all of which can be found in Fido, too, of course. But precisely inasmuch as he is a typical Irish setter, Fido shows traits which are atypical for all other dogs which are not Irish setters. This set of unique personal traits—his "typical" way of greeting me, for instance —are atypical for all the Irish setters which are not Fido. Having had some experience with dogs and in particular with Irish setters certainly has facilitated my getting acquainted with Fido: I expected him to behave in certain respects like all dogs

2. For an interesting parallel study of these, see Sigmund Freud, "The 'Uncanny,' " in *Essays on Creativity and the Unconscious* (New York, Harper Torchbooks, 1958), pp. 122–61.

behave and especially like Irish setters. Precisely to that extent, Fido was already familiar to me when I first met him; my expectations as to typical characteristics, behavior patterns, and the like, were fulfilled by his appearance and behavior. Yet, his "personal ways," say his particular food predilections, were novel, strange, unfamiliar to me.

We have indicated at an earlier place in this study[3] the inter-relationship between familiarity and typicality. We have mentioned that the world is conceived from the outset as grouped under certain types, which in turn refer to atypical aspects of the typified objects of our experiences. Types are more or less anonymous types; and, the more anonymous they are, the more objects of our experiences are conceived as partaking in the typical aspects. But at the same time, the type becomes less and less concrete; its content becomes less and less significant, that is, interpretationally relevant. As regards every type, then, anonymity and fullness of content are inversely related: the more anonymous the type the greater is the number of atypical traits which the concrete experienced object will show in its uniqueness; and the fuller the content of a type, the smaller will be the number of atypical traits, but also the smaller will be the number of objects of experience which fall under such a type.[4] We have also seen that typification is a function of the system of interpretational relevances, which in turn is determined by the topic at hand. To be sufficiently familiar with a topic means, therefore, to have established a type of such a degree of anonymity or concreteness so as to satisfy the inter-pretational requirements necessary to determine the topic at hand.

Yet, it must always be kept firmly in mind that typicality not

3. Schutz noted in the margin here the necessity to expand this analysis and later added several pages; these are attached to the present passage. Thus the phrase "at an earlier place" refers to this part of the study.

4. The implications of this relationship and other aspects of Schutz's theory to the problem of intersubjectivity have been briefly explored by R. M. Zaner, "Theory of Intersubjectivity: Alfred Schutz," *Social Research, 28* (1961), 71–93, esp. 87–93.

only refers to already acquired knowledge but at the same time to a set of expectations, especially protentions, adhering to such knowledge—namely, typicality refers to the set of expectations that future experiences will reveal these and those typical traits to the same degree of anonymity and concreteness.[5] These expectations are merely another way of expressing the general idealizations of "and so forth and so on" and "I can do it again," constitutive for the natural attitude.[6] Thus, suppose that I have accumulated sufficient "knowledge of acquaintance"[7] with a particular unique event or occurrence to have permitted me to solve a problem with respect to it and then to drop the topic. To that extent, we would say, I had familiarized myself with it sufficiently for me to come to terms with it. But as long as I have not yet grasped the typicality behind the atypical unique configuration with which I had to come to terms, I cannot store away my acquired familiar knowledge in neutralized form for later use as a habitual possession. *At least, the expectation of recurrent typical experiences is required for the full meaning of familiarity of my knowledge.* Thus, *familiarity* itself, and even knowledge in general (considered as one's habitual and dormant possession of previous experiences), *presupposes the idealizations of the "and so forth and so on" and the "I can do it again."* But these idealizations refer in this case to familiarity with the typicality of the experience—unique and therefore atypical as it was while it occurred —which typicality consists first of all in a set of expectations concerning the recurrence of typically same or similar experiences.[8]

Familiarity thus indicates the likelihood of referring new experiences, in respect of their types, to the habitual stock of

5. See *CP 3*, "Type and Eidos in Husserl's Late Philosophy," 92–115, for a fuller treatment.

6. See above, Ch. 2, n. 12.

7. Schutz is referring here to James' distinction between "knowledge about" and "knowledge of (acquaintance)." Cf. James, *Principles of Psychology, 1,* 221 f.

8. This concludes the appended passage mentioned above, n. 3.

already acquired knowledge. This reference may occur by means of a passive *synthesis of recognition.*[9] The object now actually experienced proves to be the "same," or the "same but modified," or a "like" or a "similar" object, as an object which I previously experienced, possibly many times. But this "sameness," "likeness," or "similarity" refers only to *typical* properties which the new object has in common with those I have previously experienced. It is indeed utterly impossible for me to be "through-and-through" familiar with an object of experience, precisely because every familiar object necessarily carries along with it an open horizon of hitherto unknown or strange (unfamiliar) implications and aspects that can be disclosed only in the further course of experience (which itself will reveal yet further open horizons). Any typicality ascertained in an object of our experience refers to a set of atypical properties by which this object in its uniqueness (all that which makes it be this unique object in this unique place at this unique moment) differs from all the other objects of the same type, and also from itself if experienced at other places or other moments of time. At least, this is the case for me in my natural attitude, in the context of my prevailing style of life in the everyday world in which I am not interested in the metaphysical notion of identity.

Within the context of daily life, the cathedral of Rheims is the "same" superstructure at the same spot on the surface of the earth, and the series of paintings which Monet made of this building at various times of day in different lighting refer to the same building. All these paintings show the typical traits of

9. An important and thus far unexplored convergence between Schutz and Jean Piaget should be mentioned here, especially as regards the latter's concept of "recognitory assimilation." Cf. Piaget, *The Origins of Intelligence in Children* (New York, International Universities Press, 1952), esp. pp. 35–36. Although he does not mention Schutz's work in this connection, Aron Gurwitsch's analysis of Piaget, especially on the concept of schemata, shows close parallels with Schutz's theory. Cf. Gurwitsch, *The Field of Consciousness,* esp. pp. 36–52 (and pp. 394–404 for Gurwitsch's careful explication and criticism of Schutz's theory of relevance and finite provinces of meaning).

the cathedral, familiar to any visitor or even to any student of photographic reproductions of it. However, in spite of this familiarity and typicality, and although all of these paintings were made from the same position and from the same perspective, the particular aspect of the cathedral changes in each of them. The distribution of light and shadow during the morning and in the afternoon has changed and has bestowed particular atypical and unique features on the typically familiar aspect of the well-known facade.

On the other hand, any experience which has become part of our habitual possession (and therefore familiar) carries along with it its anticipations that, as a matter of principle, certain future experiences will be recognized as referring to the same previously experienced objects, or at least to objects which are the same or typically similar to it.[10] In Carneades' example, the man who comes back to his home expects to find his room as he had left it; that is, he expects to reenter a surrounding with which he is perfectly familiar. Strictly speaking, such an expectation will necessarily be disappointed to some extent, even if no "new" object were now placed in the corner. It will be disappointed because the man left it in the morning and returned at sunset; the shadows will have changed and thus the visual shape of each of the objects in the room will have been modified. And, if the man is familiar with the typical aspect of the room at the hours of many previous sunsets, he would, when returning at this particular evening necessarily discover a set of unique atypical features—but, of course, only if he takes care to pay attention to these differences. He would then say that the objects no longer have the expected familiar aspect; to be sure, they are the same but somehow modified. Still more

10. Schutz refers here to two important phenomena: on the one hand, that of "syntheses of identification" and of "recognition," and on the other the automatically ("passively") ongoing protentions or anticipations implicit in every experience. For fuller treatments of the first, see above, Ch. 2, n. 2; for the second, see Husserl, *The Phenomenology of Inner-Time Consciousness,* pp. 76–77, 137–42, 149–54; also *Ideen 1,* Sec. 81; and Schutz, *CP 1,* "Some Leading Concepts of Phenomenology," 99–117, and "On Multiple Realities," 214–17.

strictly speaking, all other circumstances being equal, these aspects of familiar things cannot be precisely the same aspects familiar to him because his experience of their familiarity is a recurrent one. The same recurring experience, paradoxically formulated, is not the same any more precisely because it recurs. But, as we say in the language of daily life, for all practical purposes the man will find the familiar surroundings of his home the same as he had left it.

How can this paradoxical situation be explained? At this point of our inquiry, we have only to express this problem in terms of the three categories of relevance already delineated.

From this point of view, familiarity has a particular subjective meaning, namely that of *being sufficiently conversant* with an object of our experience for the actual purpose at hand. So formulated, the concept of familiarity demarcates, for the particular subject in his concretely particular life-situation, that sector of the world which does from that which does not need further investigation. The former sector may require the development of new topical and interpretational relevances, while the other sector was formerly topically and interpretationally relevant. But the task set by these previous relevances has been solved and has led to habitual knowledge, at least as to the type of experienced object in question then. It is no longer subject to further investigation (or, for my practical purposes at hand, no longer needs it), it no longer has to be questioned. Being already known (so far as my then prevailing purposes required, at least), it is to that extent beyond question and as such it is *taken for granted,*[11] an element of the now unquestioned world. But this does not mean that it is unquestionable. It is merely unquestioned until further notice, sufficiently determined for the purpose actually at hand at the time. It carries along with it, however, its outer and inner horizons of determinable indeterminacy. As long as the expectations adherent

11. Cf. *PSW,* pp. 69–74, for a fuller treatment of this crucial notion of "taken-for-grantedness": "The taken-for-granted (*das Fraglos-gegeben*) is always that particular level of experience which presents itself as not in need of further analysis." (p. 74)

to the familiar knowledge continue to be fulfilled by the typicality of supervening experiences of the same or similar objects,
as long as the world will go on as anticipated in the stock of
knowledge (i.e. of sedimented typifications), we will acquiesce
with this state of affairs. We then take things for granted until
further notice (i.e. until counterproof or until circumstances
motivate reconsideration), and we take our knowledge of them
as sufficiently assured. We are, as we say, "not interested" in
the details which are atypical either of the same object apperceived[12] in its typicality or of the class of objects, of which
the one in question is a typical instance.

We just pointed out that the realm of things taken for
granted is the outcome of activities of the mind guided by
previous topical and interpretational relevances. It is, so to
speak, their sedimentation *in the form of habitual possessions
of sufficient knowledge*. The respective contributions of these
two sets of relevances to this state of affairs is, however, different. It is the previous topical relevances which led to the
investigation of the now known objects. They are known because they were once in the thematic kernel of my field of
consciousness, topics of my questioning, problems to be solved.
In their concrete determination of what is to be put into question, these topical relevances delimited *the level up to which
the investigation had to be taken* in order to answer the question to an extent sufficient for the purposes at hand or, in other
words, to acquire sufficient familiarity with and knowledge of
the objects of experience involved. Therewith the system of all

12. Cf. *CP 1,* "Symbol, Reality and Society," esp. 294–306, for the
meaning of appresentation. As Schutz states (pp. 295–96), "if we apperceive an object of the outer world, then that which we really see in our
visual perception is merely the frontside of the object. But this perception of the visible frontside of the object involves an apperception by
analogy of the unseen backside, an apperception which, to be sure, is a
more or less empty anticipation of what we might perceive if we turned
the object around or if we walked around the object. This anticipation is
based on our past experience of normal objects of this kind [i.e. analogi-
cally] . . . Thus, by appresentation, we experience intuitively something
as indicating or depicting significantly something else." Further on in
this important article, Schutz demonstrates the crucial place of appresentation in a general theory of symbolization.

possible interpretational relevances required for the acquisition
of familiar knowledge of the topical objects was established.
As distinguished from the topical relevances, it is the previous
interpretational ones which led to the typicality of our knowledge of familiar things. Our familiarity with them is restricted
to the aspects of the objects of our experience which are interpretationally relevant for the topic at hand. These aspects are
considered to be typical of the object, typically relevant namely
for the solution of the topical problems. Each type is thus the
sum total of what is for the time being interpretationally relevant in the interpretandum.

C. Typicality and Interpretative Relevance

We enter into the outer and inner horizons of the interpretandum—the topic at hand—only so far as this investigation is
relevant for obtaining sufficient knowledge of and familiarity
with the topic. The habitual possession of familiarity thus
acquired is called our knowledge of this object of experience
in respect of its type. *The type is therefore the demarcation line
between the explored and unexplored horizons of the topic at
hand* and the outcome of formerly valid[13] systems of interpretational relevances.

It is of the greatest importance to understand how the system
of interpretational relevances functionally depends upon the
system of topical relevances. It is clear on the one hand that
there is no interpretational relevance as such, but only an interpretational relevance referring to a given topic. And as a corollary, there is no such thing as a type as such, but only types
related to particular problems, carrying, so to speak, "subscripts" referring to the topic at hand, for the interpretation of

13. What Schutz apparently has in mind here are those relevancy
systems that have already been "in use" or which have been followed,
and which are therefore "valid" in that sense. It is clearly not logical
validity he has in mind, but experiential validity, referring to those systems that have proven themselves in my previous experience and thus
may be considered operative and effective (and are now taken for
granted as such).

which they have been formed. The fundamental importance of this characteristic of types, especially for the methodology of the social sciences, will become visible in our further investigations.[14]

Husserl has already shown, in an important section of his *Erfahrung und Urteil,*[15] that the world is from the outset known in the prepredicative experience of man in the natural attitude as a world in terms of types. In the natural attitude, for instance, I do not experience percepts of outer objects of this and that configuration, Gestalt, extention, color, etc., but from the outset mountains, trees, animals, birds, dogs, fellowmen, and so on. He has clearly shown, although not in so many words, that even in the prepredicative sphere it makes a difference whether I recognize this concrete object as an animal, a mammal, a dog, an Irish setter, or "my dog Fido." In ascertaining the animal as an Irish setter, I am already *interested* in all the properties typical for the species in question, properties which are not typical for other dogs, such as greyhounds or poodles. I simply take it for granted that Irish setters, greyhounds, poodles, etc., have in common a set of typical properties and ways of behaving which characterize the genus "dog" and make each member of it distinguishable from other mammals such as "cats." To speak of Fido as a mammal is to say that I am interested in the typical properties and ways of behaving common to all kinds of dogs, cats, and many other animals—that they give birth to infants, nourish them with milk, etc.

D. Interest and Motivational Relevance

But what does "interest" mean in such cases? Obviously, it refers to the system of motivational relevances which induced me to make a certain aspect of the object in question the topic of my investigation or concern. *Interest in this sense is the set*

14. This connection is not examined in the present study but is brought out in his posthumous study, *Die Strukturen der Lebenswelt.*
15. Cf. Husserl, *Erfahrung und Urteil,* Secs. 83 (a) and (b).

of motivational relevances which guide the selective activity of my mind. These relevances may be either actually operative when I turn to an "intrinsic topic," or they may be present as the sediment of relevances which were formerly actually operative in a neutralized form, namely as habitual possessions of my stock of knowldege. In the latter case, the neutralized motivational relevances are, so to speak, dormant but ready to be activated at any time to meet the challenge of the actual circumstances (as defined by my biographical situation at any particular moment of my life). Still, two terms used here are still not sufficiently clear.

1. We have used the term "intrinsic topic" in our description of interest as originating in motivational relevances: are imposed relevances also motivationally determined? This question cannot be properly answered at this stage of the analysis. Anticipating later results, nevertheless, we may say that imposed relevances of all kinds are indeed connected with interest (whether it originates in active or dormant motivational relevances). But, we will see, *imposed relevances are a derived type of intrinsic relevance; they are so to speak relevances of a second order.*

2. We also spoke of the actual circumstances as defined by my biographical situation at any given moment. We shall have to devote a part of our later discussion to the clarification of this. For now it is sufficient to note that at any moment of our life, consciousness is focused on a certain sector of the world which is determined by the sum total of motivational relevances of all kinds—and this we may call my "heed" or "interest."

Motivational relevances, we have seen, are of two kinds. On the one hand are the in-order-to type, which are arranged into a particular hierarchy and are interrelated (if not integrated) with one another into what is commonly called a "plan": plan for thought and for action, for work and for leisure, for the present hour or for the week, and so on. Each of these, in turn, are interrelated (but not necessarily integrated) into a general, paramount plan: the plan for life. These in-order-to motivations, however, are founded on a set of genuine because motives sedimented in the biographically determined situation of the self at a particular moment. Psychologists have various names for this set of because motives: attitudes, personality traits, and even character. We prefer the term motivational relevances, keeping in mind that this term covers manifold but interrelated features.

E. The Stock of Knowledge at Hand

To sum up: we have found that what we call our stock of knowledge at hand is the sedimentation of various previous activities of our mind, and these are guided by systems of prevailing actually operative relevances of different kinds. These activities lead to the acquisition of habitual knowledge which is dormant, neutralized, but ready at any time to be re-activated. Motivational relevances lead to the constitution of the "interest" situation, which in turn determines the system of topical relevances. The latter bring material which was horizonal or marginal into the thematic field, thus determining the problems for thought and action for further investigation, selected from the background which is, ultimately, the world which is beyond question and taken for granted. These topical relevances also determine the level or limits for such investigation required for producing knowledge and familiarity sufficient for the problem at hand. Thus, the system of interpretational relevances becomes established, and this leads to the determination of the typicality structure of our knowledge.

These interrelationships among the types of relevances should not be taken as chronological, that "first" the one, "then" the other, "then" the last type becomes established. All three types are concretely experienced as inseparable, or at least as an undivided unity, and their dissection from experience into three types is the result of an analysis of their constitutive origin. Living in its acts, says Husserl, the mind is directed exclusively toward its objects of action or thought. To bring the performed activity into view it is necessary artificially to perform an act of reflection; only thereby can the flux of experiences be grasped as such.[16]

The same holds for the systems of relevances. In our mental activities[17] we are directed exclusively toward the theme of the field of consciousness—that is, toward the problem we are concerned with, the object of our interest or attention, in short toward the topical relevances. Everything else is in the margin, the horizon, and especially all the habitual possessions we have called the stock of knowledge at hand. The motives for our actions are also in the margin of the field, whether the motives be of the in-order-to type (beyond or before the topically relevant theme) or the because type (which belongs essentially to our past and leads to the building up of the chain of in-order-to motives governing the determination of the theme or topic).

16. But, as Husserl points out, such reflection in no way necessarily distorts or obliterates the experiential unity reflected upon. To be sure, insofar as one reflects (say, on an act of perception) he is no longer *straightforwardly* "living-in" his perceiving consciousness, attentive to the objects being perceived, but is rather living-in his *reflection* on his act of perception. In this sense, Husserl states that "an essentially changed subjective process [*Erlebnis*] takes the place of the original one" and thus alters it (that is, reflection takes the place of the perception and therefore, by replacing it, modifies it; it is no longer characterized by ego-activity, among other things). But this is *only* to say that instead of being straightforwardly concerned with worldly objects (through perception), one is now reflectively concerned with acts and their objects-as-experienced through these acts. Thus, Husserl continues, "The proper task of reflection however is not to repeat the original process, but to consider it and explicate what can be found in it." (*Cartesian Meditations,* 34; see also 46.) This point is quite crucial inasmuch as some philosophers would have it that *any* reflection must alter, in the sense of essentially distort and/or destroy, what is reflected upon —a point that rests on a serious confusion between the act of reflection and what is reflected upon. Cf., e.g., Merleau-Ponty, *Phénoménologie de la perception* (Paris, Librairie Gallimard, 1945), pp. 261 f., 275 ff., passim (Eng. trans. by Colin Smith [London, Routledge and Kegan Paul, Ltd., 1962], pp. 226 f., 238 ff., passim); and Sartre, *L'Être et le néant,* pp. 198–202 (E.T., pp. 151–55). Cf. R. Zaner, *The Problem of Embodiment,* Phaenomenologica 17 (The Hague, Martinus Nijhoff, 1964), 107–11, 199–204.

17. Schutz speaks here of "metal" activities, but surely this is unnecessarily narrow in this context, since his point concerns "working" activities as well.

And, of course, implicit in the inner and outer horizons of the topic are those elements which become interpretationally relevant in the ongoing course of the activity of our mind as regards the topically relevant thematic center or kernel. It is also obvious that I may at any time turn to what is implicit or hidden in these horizons (to what is in the margin of the field) and bring such elements into the thematic kernel (i.e. make thematic what has been only operative or marginal). Indeed, I may do this without letting what was formerly topically relevant out of my grip. If I do keep it "in grip,"[18] it may continue to subsist as the main topic in relation to which the formerly horizonal elements, now brought into the thematic kernel, are constituted as subtopics or subthemes having manifold relations (of foundedness, contiguity, modification and modalization) to the main theme or topic.

F. The Interdependence of the Three Systems of Relevance

In terms of the point of view of the person directed toward the main topic of his interest—i.e. "subjectively"—it is therefore perfectly possible to experience the three main types of relevances in quite a different chronological sequence than seemed to be implied in our delineation above. Indeed, we may safely state that any of the three systems of relevance might be experienced as the point of departure in time—so to speak, as home base. This can be briefly illustrated by cases involving the emergence of an unfamiliar aspect of a familiar experience, or even of a strange, that is, entirely novel experience.

It is the main characteristic of all habitual possessions, that is of the knowledge we take for granted as beyond question (whether it be familiarity of thinking or of practice which is involved), that they carry along with themselves expectations of the "and so on and so forth" or the "I can do it again" type—expectations, that is, that the same or the typically similar experiences will recur. We may for instance expect that the un-

18. Schutz here refers back to Ch. 2, Sec. C for related discussion on topical relevance.

seen other side of a red sphere now perceived from "this" side will be red and spherical if we turn the object around (or if we walk around it). This expectation corresponds to our habitual knowledge pertaining to the typical similarity of front and back sides of typically similar objects. But this expectation may or may not be fulfilled. It may happen that the unseen back side, once made visible, turns out not to be red but spotty, and not to be spherical but deformed.

In general terms, it might be that the anticipated typicality of the recurrent, hitherto unquestioned state of affairs turns out to be otherwise than anticipated, that the anticipation is frustrated (or disconfirmed) by the emergent atypicality of the anticipated event, or that a routine activity we are performing is hampered by an unforeseen obstacle. The thing, event, or state of affairs may turn out to be "otherwise than expected," seeing "not this but something else." It is precisely this "not so but otherwise" which gives the new experience the character of being an unfamiliar one. "How strange! Things do not go on as they used to up until now! They cannot be taken for granted any longer!" Here is the counterproof which invalidates the hitherto unquestioned course of experience. What emerges as a strange experience, then, needs to be investigated, *if it is interesting enough,* because of its very unfamiliarity. It has become questionable. And therewith new topical relevances arise.

In such a case there is clearly present a twofold relationship between the systems of topical and motivational relevances. On the one hand, it is the prevailing system of motivational relevances, my evoked interest, which leads to the constitution of the new topical relevance: namely, to investigate the atypical, the strange event which proves to be a "not so but otherwise." On the other hand, the newly created topical relevance may be the origin and starting point of a set of new motivational relevances. Something formerly irrelevant (because just implied in the unexplored horizon of the familiar main topic) has now become interesting and has been constituted as a new topic or at least as a new subtopic. It is still unfamiliar to me, but having now become topically relevant it "incites me" (that is, it becomes motivationally relevant to me) to "familiarize myself" with it. I may for instance try to refer the unfamiliar experience to previously experienced affairs. I decide to do so by entering into the as yet unexplored and therefore strange horizons of the matters which were hitherto taken to be irrelevant and thus not "worth" investigation. After all, did I not believe that I was up until now sufficiently familiar with the object in question—"sufficient," that is, for my purposes at hand prevailing up until now? It may be, of course, that I will find in these unexplored horizons some indications referring to anticipations of elements or occurrences which, although atypical in terms of what has thus far been familiar to me, will have "something to do" with the strange and unfamiliar experience.

Now, in order to transform horizonal implications of the main topic into subtopics, I must continuously modify my system of interpretational relevances, those which bear "subscripts" as regards the main topic prevailing thus far. On the other hand, it is quite possible that a shift in the system of interpretational relevances—as with the introduction of a new concept—becomes the starting point for building up a set of new motivational or topical relevances which do not thus far pertain to the familiar stock of knowledge at hand.

Our study thus shows that we cannot bestow a privileged position upon one of the three systems of relevances. On the contrary, any of them may become the starting point for bringing about changes in the other two. We may graphically represent this circular interrelationship by the following diagram:

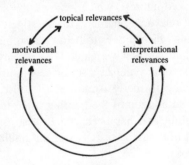

topical relevances

motivational
relevances

interpretational
relevances

The three systems of relevances are therefore but three aspects of a single set of phenomena.

Nevertheless, we believe that the distinctions we have drawn among the three is more than merely hair-splitting; it is hoped that the following investigation will prove its usefulness. Anticipating some of our results, we may say that the theory of *topical relevances* will contribute to a clarification of *the concept of value* and of our freedom in selecting the values by which we want to be guided in our theoretical and practical lives. Furthermore, the theory of *interpretational relevances* will shed a new light on the *function and meaning of methodology* (which is restricted to the realm of interpretational relevances) and furnish the foundation of a theory of expectation and especially of problems of rationalization. This second theory will also prove to be extremely helpful in the *clarification of the theory of verification, invalidation, and falsification of propositions* relating to empirical facts, and as well will contribute to the *constitutive problems of typicality.* The theory of *motivational relevances,* finally, will be found helpful for the analysis of problems correlated with *personality structure* and especially for the theory of *intersubjective understanding.*[19]

G. Shortcomings of this Presentation; Reference to Further Problems

Before proceeding, however, several omissions must be noted. The preceding analysis of the familiarity and strangeness of typical and atypical aspects of known things, of relating new experiences to the stock of knowledge at hand, disregarded the important problem concerning the *emergent novel experience* —i.e. the experience of something absolutely unknown up until now and incapable of being correlated with the prevailing stock of knowledge at hand except insofar as it cannot be subsumed under it (not even under one of the typifications in terms of which I have up until now grouped and organized the world

19. Schutz did not get to these "results" in the present study.

around me). We wish to reserve the term "novel" for experiences of this kind, those which can become known only by means of a radical modification of the systems of relevances prevailing up to the moment of their emergence. The novel experience will have to fill a vacancy in our stock of knowledge at hand. This problem of vacancies in our knowledge leads into new dimensions of our investigation and will be analyzed in the next two chapters of this study.[20]

But our preceding analysis also suffers from other shortcomings, due to the attempt to simplify the presentation of a most complicated matter.

1. We must first of all add that our stock of knowledge at hand not only encompasses the sedimentations of our previous mental activities (guided by the then prevailing systems of relevances), but also that these systems themselves are, as habitual possessions, elements of the stock of knowledge at hand. And although they may be unquestioned and taken for granted, they are always capable of becoming topically relevant for further investigation. We may, for instance, ask ourselves whether one or another of our interests is "worth bothering with," whether we are "seeing things in their proper light," or whether we have "the right attitude to our problems." These examples are borrowed from the language of daily life, but they recur in the methods of science on another level, as when a scientist asks himself whether the problem he is pursuing is a genuine one or whether he is using the right method for interpreting the facts at hand. In such cases, these matters may remain merely marginal or become topically relevant and thereby themes of new experiences.

2. Moreover, it has to be kept in mind that our stock of knowledge at hand not only contains habitual possessions originating in our theoretical activities, but also it contains our habitual ways of practical thinking and acting (e.g. ways for solving practical problems), habitual ways and patterns of behaving, acting, working, and so on. The stock of knowledge at

20. The analysis of "vacancies" or enclaves (*Leerstelle*) is given especially in Ch. 6, Sec. B (3) and (4).

hand includes, therefore, the set of practical recipes for attaining typical ends by typical means—recipes which have "stood the test" thus far and are therefore taken for granted. This omission in our analysis is due to the fact that before integrating the world of action into our system, we have to study separately the various forms of human action, a task to be taken up in the second part of this study.[21]

3. Closely connected with that problem is another, correlated with the various dimensions of reality in which we live, their time and meaning structures: namely, the problem of the *performability of our actions within the ontological structure of the world*. Such questions also refer to elements of our stock of knowledge at hand. They have been thus far disregarded because we have naïvely assumed that the reality of the world we live in has simply one unanalyzed dimension. Only our investigation of the nature of human action in Part II of this study will enable us to determine the world of working as the paramount reality from which all the other dimensions of reality can be derived.[22] The problem of relevance will therefore have to be investigated again with respect to the multiple dimensions of reality and the particular time-dimensions involved therein. This will be done in Part IV, which will finally clarify the distinctions between imposed and intrinsic relevances.

4. The most critical omission made thus far refers to the fact that we have handled our problem—and will in this and the following part continue to do so—as if there were no social world at all, as if an isolated individual experienced the world of nature disconnected from his fellowmen. Since the clarification of the problems of the social world in both aspects, as the world we naïvely live in and as the subject matter of the social sciences, is the main goal of our study, it is obvious that this omission was only made for the sake of a simplified presentation of the problems involved. The third part of this study will

21. Not included in the present study.
22. For more detailed treatment of these issues, see *CP 1,* "On Multiple Realities," 207–59, "Common-Sense and Scientific Interpretation of Human Action," 3–47, and "Choosing Among Projects of Action," 67–96.

be devoted to the study of the manifold relationships between man and fellowman, the problems of communication, the various forms of social and cultural organization as experienced by men living naïvely with others in the world taken for granted not only by him but also by others. The concept of relevances and their interdependencies will have to be revised completely as soon as the concept of intersubjectivity is introduced. The world as taken for granted is not my private world, nor, for the most part, are the systems of relevances. Knowledge is from the outset socialized knowledge, and thus, too, are the systems of relevances and the world as taken for granted. We shall have to anticipate some of the results of these later inquiries when we take up the problem of the biographically determined situation of the self[23]—which cannot be even partially analyzed without reference to the problem of intersubjectivity.

For the time being, nevertheless, we have to continue our investigation on a more simplified and restricted level. We shall begin with an analysis of the concept of our stock of knowledge at hand, both genetically and statically, which will give us the occasion to clarify the concept of the world as taken for granted.

23. See below, Ch. 7.

A. Introduction: The Heterogeneous Character of the Stock of Knowledge at Hand as the Outcome of Sedimentation

As we have seen, what we call our stock of knowledge at hand has its history, which can be interpreted as the sedimentation of previous experiences. Yet there is no primordial experience upon which all subsequent knowledge could possibly be founded. If we analyze the constitutive process of sedimentation of our knowledge which is actually at hand, we are always led to a preceding biographically determined situation with its pertinent stock of knowledge then at hand—but never to a first experience (first in the chronological sense or in the sense of foundation) which would be constitutive for all following experiences.

In this and the next chapter we have to study the structural organization of our stock of knowledge at hand in two ways. On the one hand, we must investigate the various categories of our knowledge in terms of which consciousness experiences the world at any particular moment. Along with this, we need to raise the question concerning the extent to which the unknown is delineated by the known—that is, the problem of aporetics. This study will yield a *static analysis* of the stock of knowledge at hand at a given moment. On the other hand, we must examine more closely than we have thus far the constitutive processes which led to the sedimentation of previous experiences into what is now called the stock of knowledge at hand. This study is a *genetic analysis*.[1]

We propose to begin our investigation with the latter analysis for the following reason: certain outstanding features of the actual stock of knowledge at hand, statically interpreted, can only be understood through an analysis of the constitutive processes of which they are the outcome. Without having any ambition to discuss the problems of the constitutional analysis of consciousness completely—a task which only a fully developed phenomenology of constitution could accomplish— we are exclusively concerned with some of those events in the process of sedimentation of knowledge that lead to a particular typicality of the sediment itself. One special problem, that concerning the constitutive processes relating to the systems of relevance, was discussed in the previous section. We must now investigate some other features of the process of sedimentation.

B. *Degrees of Plausibility and* diexodos

The stock of knowledge at hand at any particular moment of our conscious lives is by no means homogeneous or integrated. Its elements are neither consistent in themselves or necessarily compatible with one another. They are arranged in various degrees of plausibility ($\pi\iota\theta\alpha\nu\delta s$) from the conviction of certainty through all the modalizations of opinion, including that of blind belief or indifference in which "I let things stand as they are." For our purpose, therefore, knowledge means not only explicit, clarified, well-formulated insight, but also all forms of opinion and acceptance[2] relating to a state of affairs as taken for granted. For the time being, we restrict ourselves to showing that the heterogeneous character of the *various elements of our stock of knowledge* can be explained by the *various processes leading to their sedimentation*. Only a few of these ele-

1. See Husserl, *Cartesian Meditations,* Secs. 37–39, 48, 61, for his notion of "static" and "genetic" analysis.
2. Schutz's term is "acquiescence." "Acceptance" seems preferable inasmuch as Schutz is here concerned with doxic (opinion) or epistemic states of affairs.

ments are assured by the process which Carneades calls *periodeusis,* and even fewer by what he calls *diexodos.*

Some of these elements are accepted as plausible because our first experience of a particular object has not been put in question or doubt by subsequent experiences either of the same object or of its interrelatedness with other objects. Other experiences (or their objects) were put into question and led to a situation of doubting, but this process of questioning or doubting (the process of *periodeuein)* did not lead to any decision, to an assent to one of the problematic alternatives, and perhaps not even to the establishment of a genuine problematic alternative. This process was for some reason interrupted—such as the object in question disappeared or was covered up by another one; or by means of a shift of the prevailing system of relevances, my "interest" in following up the further investigation discontinued.

With respect to still other elements I may have accomplished the diexodos: genuine alternatives, originating in a situation of doubt, "stood to choice," each of them having its own weight. I came to a decision, thus giving my assent to one of them. Yet the term of the alternative not assented to was, so long as it stood to choice, believed to be equally plausible. By making my decision, this belief in the plausibility of the rejected term was "stricken out," "annihilated," or has at least been dropped. The other term, however, became transformed by my very assent into a conviction of its plausibility which I feel entitled to consider as well-founded, although merely well-founded "until further notice."

The last mentioned case (the accomplished diexodos) is obviously what Husserl calls *empirical certainty*—which, according to him, is always a certainty until counterproof, or until further notice.[3] In all the other cases, in which the diexodos was not accomplished, my belief in the plausibility of the knowledge achieved does not have the character of empirical

3. Cf. Husserl, *Ideen 1,* Secs. 104 and 105; and *Erfahrung und Urteil,* Sec. 77. Schutz discusses these issues in some depth in *CP 1,* "Choosing Among Projects of Action," esp. 77–82.

certainty but merely of *empirical likelihood,* of empirical
chance. And such likelihood or chance has many degrees: my
belief is then not a well-founded conviction but a mere opinion,
presumption, trust, or (to use Santayana's term) mere animal
faith. It might be a matter of having no foundation at all, and
would then be a sense like "as far as I know," or "I have reason
to believe," or "subject to further investigation," or "it is my
impression," or "I presume," or even "I do not care what this
may be."

In this way the various degrees of plausibility of the elements
of the stock of knowledge at hand originate in the historical
processes which lead to them—i.e. in the process of sedimentation.

C. *Polythetic and Monothetic Reflection*

The acquisition of knowledge of any form is a process in time
which is articulated in various steps. The various phases which,
according to Carneades, the man runs through in building up
his knowledge of what is plausible—from the uncertain representation through its "being bent," from periodeusis to diexodos
—are such steps leading to the acquisition of knowledge and
take place within the inner time of the flux of consciousness.
The interplay between the various systems of relevance—from
the motivational interest, for example, to the building up of a
topically relevant theme and the full development of the interplay of interpretational relevances leading to the determination
of the typicality of our knowledge—is another example. When
we enter gradually into the inner and outer horizons of the
topically relevant theme, bringing more and more material from
the horizonal margin into the thematic focus (making the manifold implications hidden in the horizon increasingly explicit),
we are engaged in a process consisting of many separate steps
of mental activity which lead to the sedimentation of our
habitual possession called knowledge at hand.

These examples (which might be interpreted as referring to
experiences occurring at the prepredicative level) have, of

course, their corollary in the cognitive sphere proper, namely in the sphere of predicative positing, of propositions, judgments, and inferences—in brief, of thinking in terms of formal logic.[4] Strictly speaking, any explicit predicating, as in the formulating of the proposition, *"S is p,"* is already a process in time; it is a kind of dissection of an undivided experience (such as "The-pack-of-cards-is-on-the-table," as William James so graphically describes the situation)[5] into the single conceptual elements contained therein and the various relations prevailing among these elements. As will be explained at a later point in this study, the apparently simple proposition, *"S is p,"* is merely an abbreviation for the proposition, *"S is, among many other things, such as p, r, . . . x, y, z, also p,"* it being understood that in emphasizing the *p*-ness of *S* one is not interested in its other aspects, qualities, or properties (*q, r, x, y,* etc.)[6] This selection of the "interesting" aspects from all the possible ones—which is, incidentally, closely connected with the interplay of the three systems of relevance—is itself a process leading to the result of predicative positing.

The problem under scrutiny will become fully comprehensible if we turn to chains of propositions, judgments, and inferences as used in scientific reasoning. The Pythagorean theorem, for instance, is deducible step by step from Euclid's axioms and theorems derived from these. It was in just this way that we all learned to prove the proposition, $a^2 + b^2 = c^2$. In order to grasp the meaning of the theorem, however, it is not necessary to repeat the single steps by which it was derived or proven. Indeed, we might have even forgotten the way in which it can be proved and still know that in a rectangular

4. The concern of formal logic is the sphere of predication generally; that of "transcendental logic," on the other hand, is the sphere of the prepredicative generally. Cf. Husserl, *Formale und transzendentale Logik*.

5. Cf. William James, *Principles of Psychology, 1,* 240. See also Schutz, *CP 3,* "William James' Concept of the Stream of Thought Phenomenologically Interpreted," 1–14.

6. Cf. *CP 1,* "Common-Sense and Scientific Interpretation of Human Action," esp. 8–9, and "Choosing Among Projects of Action," esp. 75–77.

triangle the sum of the squares of the sides including the right
angle equals the square of the hypotenuse. This proposition,
derived in the various steps of deduction, has become a habitual
possession of our stock of knowledge, whereas the single steps
of the deduction have been forgotten. More precisely, these
steps are "out of our grip" but still dormant, present in our
knowledge in a neutralized way but able to be awakened and reactivated.

All these examples are merely illustrations of a general principle which, according to Husserl, governs the reflective attitude
by which consciousness may grasp the meaning of its past experiences. "Living in the acts" of my mental activities, I am
directed merely toward the state of affairs to be brought about
by these activities, not toward these activities themselves.[7] In
order to grasp the meaning of the activities, I must turn to them
in a reflective attitude. I must, as Dewey expresses it, stop and
think.[8] I am then no longer immersed and carried along by my
stream of consciousness; I must step out of the stream and
look at it. Of course, all these terms are merely metaphors, and
even dangerous ones, for there is no flux which I could possibly step out of; my very looking at it is itself an event within
the stream. Any attempt to translate phenomena of inner time,
of *durée,* into spatial terms are, as Bergson saw so clearly, un-
fortunate and misleading.[9] But taking this precaution, our
metaphor might give a graphic account of the phenomenon of
reflection, although we cannot give a full account of it within
the limits of the present study.[10]

There are two ways in which the mind may grasp the meaning of its own previous experiences. All of them are built up
step by step, phase by phase, in processes of inner time—
"polythetically," as Husserl says.[11] I may in the reflective at-

7. See above, Ch. 3, n. 16; cf. also *PSW,* pp. 47, 51–53. For the
Husserlian distinction, see *Ideen 1,* Secs. 77, 78, 101.

8. See *CP 1,* "On Multiple Realities," 214–15.

9. Cf. Bergson, *Les données immédiates de la conscience,* pp. 136
f., 142 ff., 174–80 (E.T., pp. 181 f., 190 ff., 232–40).

10. See *PSW,* pp. 45–53; and Ch. 3, n. 16.

11. For Husserl's distinction between polythetic and monothetic, see
above, Ch. 2, n. 16.

titude reconstruct this polythetic building up of the meaning
of my experience upon which I now direct my reflective glance.
I may reconstruct the process in memory, again run through
all the steps and phases in and by which the meaning of my
experience became constituted. I *may* do so—at least under
ideal conditions, that is, disregarding all obstacles and disturbances arising from the particular situation—with respect
to all kinds of meaningful experiences. Indeed, I *must* choose
this procedure if the meaning of the experience in question
consists exclusively in the polythetic arrangements of elements
in inner time, as it is the case in music and poetry and other
forms of so-called time-immanent objects *(Zeitgegenstände).*[12]
I can reproduce the meaning of a work of music merely by
reproducing its flux (at least mentally) from the first bar to the
last; I may render the "content" of a poem in one or two sentences, and this is just what the glosses of the "Ancient Mari-
ner" do. Yet in order to grasp the meaning of the poem as such,
I have to read or recite it, at least mentally—and that is to reconstruct polythetically the many articulated (i.e. polythetic)
steps in which its meaning has been constituted.[13]

Apart from these cases of time-immanent objects, however,
and especially with respect to experiences which are con-
ceptually formulated by a process of ratiocination, I may grasp
in a single ray—monothetically, as Husserl calls it[14]—the
meaning which has been built up polythetically. In this case,
my habitual possession of knowledge consists in the experienced meaning as monothetically grasped.

The distinction between polythetic and monothetic grasping
of the meaning of our experience is a fundamental insight into
the texture of mental life, one which we shall encounter frequently. Its vital importance for the structure of our stock
of knowledge at hand is obvious. The clarity and distinctness of
our knowledge depends upon the possibility of our being able

12. For further details, see *PSW*, pp. 48–55, esp. the relevant references to Husserl's *Phenomenology of Inner-Time Consciousness,* 51–52,
184.
13. Cf. *PSW*, pp. 68–78.
14. See above, Ch. 2, n. 16.

to refer the monothetically grasped meaning of an element of
our knowledge to the polythetic steps by which such knowledge
was acquired.[15] The degree of plausibility of our knowledge,
from our conviction of empirical certainty to blind belief (in
addition to other factors), will be determinable according as
this knowledge was acquired by clear and distinct steps which
can be polythetically reconstructed. In ordinary language: it
depends upon whether we can account for the source of knowledge by indicating the single acts of becoming aware, conceiv-
ing, understanding, apprehending, and learning by which we
become cognizant of or acquainted with an element of our
knowledge.

We may also translate the distinction between polythetic
and monothetic knowledge into terms of relevance structure.
The habitual possession of knowledge grasped merely monothetically disregards the system of motivational relevances
(both the in-order-to and the because relevances) which lead to
the establishment of topical relevances. The distinction between
topical and interpretational relevances is, so to speak, pre-
historical for the monothetic grasping of the habitually possessed knowledge at hand. To look monothetically at the meaning of one of our experiences clearly indicates a shift in the
configuration of our systems of relevances prevailing at the time
of its polythetic constitution. Then, the topically relevant
thematic kernel required bringing horizonal interpretational
material into the center of the field—what was marginal, say,
at the first step of the polythetic process became thematic when
the second was carried out, what was implied in the inner
horizon during the second step became explicit by performing
the third, and so on. At any step, the interpretational relevances
and, therewith, the typicality of the approached object of our
experience was modified, and all these processes were continued until the problem at hand was sufficiently clarified and
solved (sufficiently, that is, for the purpose at hand)—only
when this process comes to a standstill can the meaning-structure then built up polythetically be grasped monothetically.

15. Schutz marked this sentence unsatisfactory.

This standstill may be achieved either if the whole process ended in the solution of the problem at hand or if it was interrupted, dropped,[16] or if, even without having arrived at a solution, I turn reflexively to the polythetic steps thus far performed and look at them in one single way (monothetically)—thus grasping the meaning of my experiencing act as thus far developed.

In all these cases, however, a reinterpretation of the monothetically grasped steps occurs with respect to their place in the various systems of relevance. The monothetically grasped material shows typicality other than that in each of the steps in which it was built up polythetically, because the interpretational relevances changed as we proceeded and now are different when the process came in one way or another to a standstill. What was topically relevant while polythetically proceeding from step to step becomes at best a subtopic in the new topical relevance of the habitual possession grasped monothetically. It may also have lost its relevance completely and prove to have been only of auxiliary relevance with respect to the newly constituted monothetic main topic. Variations of all kinds are possible but they all refer to the interplay of formerly operative motivational relevances now set aside or discarded.

This distinction between polythetically and monothetically grasped elements of our knowledge will become of special im· portance in the study of three problems which are more closely interconnected than it may at first glance appear.

1. The meaning-structure of our actions in the sense of projected conduct for the purpose of solving a certain theoretical or practical problem is clarified by the distinction. In order to bring about the state of affairs aimed at, to project it and delimit thereby the goal of our action, to ascertain the means appropriate for achieving this end, to decide whether the means are within my reach or accessible to me and therewith the goal of action performable, and finally to carry out this action either within the paramount reality of the world of

16. See below, Ch. 5.

working or the theoretical reality of pure thinking—for all these steps, a certain reference to being known, habitually possessed, or made topically relevant for the performing of each of these steps is required. It will be of the greatest importance to analyze the polythetic steps by which the project becomes built up—the project whose meaning is monothetically grasped while the action intended to actualize it is carried out. The carrying out of the ongoing action in turn can be grasped polythetically. But the already performed action has, to both actor and observer, a monothetic meaning which need not (and strictly speaking *cannot*) coincide with the monothetic meaning of the project before the action has been carried out.[17]

2. Our knowledge is socially derived and distributed.[18] Only a very small part of my stock of knowledge at hand originates in my own personal experience of things. By far the greater part is socially derived, originating in the experiences of others, communicated to me by others, or handed down to me by my parents or my teachers, or the teachers of my teachers. All of this knowledge derived from others, believed by me in various degrees of plausibility, becomes my own habitual possession of things known—frequently just taken over by me without question, i.e. simply monothetically grasped without any attempt by me to perform any polythetic reconstruction of the steps leading to the monothetically grasped meaning. My friend "knows what he is talking about," and I rely on him and just typically take it for granted without question that what he tells me is the case. But even if I attempted to break down socially derived knowledge into polythetic steps, it may frequently turn out that these traditional, habitual items of knowledge are such only as regards the monothetic meaning pertaining to the things supposedly known, whereas the tradition which contains the polythetic steps leading to this sedimentation (i.e. to the monothetic meaning) has been lost. It may even be that polythetic steps of this kind were never performed and

17. Cf. *PSW*, pp. 86–98, 104.
18. Cf. *CP 1*, "Common-Sense and Scientific Interpretation of Human Action," esp. 13–15.

that the socially derived knowledge is based on the authority of a philosopher or hero or saint or the blind belief incorporated in the "idols of the tribe." The origin of the folkways and mores in the sense in which Sumner uses these[19] consists in the socially derived monothetic knowledge without discernible polythetic foundations.

3. Yet any form of socially derived knowledge presupposes communication, and this in turn is only possible by human interaction gearing into the outer world through, e.g., movements of one's lips. These occurrences in the outer world take place in a series of polythetic steps. To take spoken language as an example of communication: the speaker builds up, word by word, sentence by sentence, the polythetic meaning-content he wants to convey by his speech. The listener follows this process polythetically. On the other hand, even before starting his speech, the speaker may monothetically look at the meaning of the thought he wants to convey, and the listener, although never quite sure where the sentence started by the speaker will lead before it is completed, may grasp by a monothetic glance the meaning of the other's thought (and may even, while the process is going on, anticipate, although in a vague and empty way, "what he is about to say"). All of this will have to be studied carefully later on.[20]

Generally speaking, however, what we stated concerning communication by language with respect to polythetic and monothetic meaning-structure holds good not only for any kind of communication but also for the interpretation of the actions of our fellowmen in general. We may always polythetically grasp the ongoing phases of the other's ongoing actions and monothetically grasp the meaning of this action in both respects, i.e. the meaning it has for him, the actor, and for us, his partners or observers. We cannot at this point of our study enter

19. William G. Sumner, *Folkways, A Study of the Sociological Importance of Manners, Customs, Mores and Morals* (New York, Ginn and Company, 1906).

20. Not included in the present study, but see *PSW*, Secs. 19–27; also *CP 2*, "The Dimensions of the Social World," 20–63, and "Making Music Together," 159–78.

into the detailed description of our understanding of the actions of our fellowmen; this will be handled extensively in Part III.[21] We may only venture to say here that the distinction between polythetic and monothetic meaning-structure will turn out to be a key concept not only for our knowledge of our fellowman's action, but also for the understanding of our fellowman and the whole structurization of our social world.

D. Units of Meaning-Context

Yet the possibility of grasping the polythetic steps by which a monothetic meaning-structure is built up has certain essential limits. William James has already discovered the particular articulation of our stream of consciousness which he describes, comparing it with the flight of a bird, as flying stretches and resting places.[22] Aron Gurwitsch has shown in a remarkable paper the importance of this theory for the foundation of Gestalt psychology.[23]

It is a peculiarity of the mind that its activities cannot be broken down beyond certain limits; it is impossible to "atomize" this unit without running into paradoxes and antinomies impossible to solve. The reason for this phenomenon can be understood by means of Bergson's theory of inner time.[24] The *durée* cannot be decomposed into quantitatively homogeneous units. There is no yardstick for intensities; only space can be decomposed into measurable limits of extension. But even in space the phenomenon of motion, partaking equally in time and

21. Not included in the present study, but see above, n. 20, and *CP 1,* "Scheler's Theory of Intersubjectivity and the General Thesis of the Alter Ego," 150–79, "Sartre's Theory of the Alter Ego," 180–203, "Symbol, Reality and Society," esp. 312–39; and *CP 3,* "The Problem of Transcendental Intersubjectivity in Husserl," 51–83.

22. Cf. James, *Principles of Psychology, 1,* 245–71; also Aron Gurwitsch, *Studies in Phenomenology and Psychology* (Evanston, Northwestern University Press, 1966), "William James' Theory of the 'Transitive Parts' of the Stream of Consciousness," pp. 301–33.

23. Cf. ibid., "Some Aspects and Developments of Gestalt Psychology," pp. 3–55, and "The Phenomenological and the Psychological Approach to Consciousness," pp. 89–106.

24. Cf. Bergson, *Les données immédiates de la conscience,* Ch. 1 and pp. 56–90 (E. T., Ch. 1 and pp. 74–121); also *Matière et mémoire,* pp. 213 ff. (E. T., pp. 250 ff.).

space, cannot be dissolved into homogeneous units without sub-
stituting "space-run-through" for "ongoing movement." If
we try to break down the unified act of ongoing motion into
the units of space-run-through by supposing that the latter is
identical with the former, then, indeed, the arrow shot from
the bow will never reach its target but remain motionless in
mid-air—Achilles will never overhaul the turtle, and the Eleatic
paradoxes will remain irrefutable. It seems that in discussing
the phenomenon of stretches of flight and resting places of
consciousness, we have to handle two different aspects of it:
(1) How is it possible that our attempt to break down our
experiences into smaller units is impossible beyond certain
limits? (2) What constitutes such units as being indivisible?
What creates the articulation of our stream of consciousness?

Both aspects refer clearly to the *meaning-context within
which our experiences stand for us from the outset*. It was the
error of the old tabula rasa theory of mind and the association-
istic psychology based upon this assumption to argue that we
have isolated perceptions, ideas, sentiments, following one
another in time, by which our knowledge of the world is built
up—an error, however, which is most understandable. Modern
psychological theories, especially that of Gestalt psychology,
have refuted this erroneous theory at the level of psychology
of perception.[25] And modern theories of the functioning of the
organism, especially the discoveries by Goldstein[26] in connection with language disturbances due to brain lesions, have
furnished counterevidence at the biological level. Finally, the
new concepts of the relationships between meaning-structure
and inner time in the philosophies of William James, Bergson,
and Husserl have laid the foundations for a constitutive analysis of consciousness.[27] Without entering here into a detailed

25. For a thorough and searching critique of these theories, see Gurwitsch, *The Field of Consciousness,* Parts I and II.

26. See Kurt Goldstein, *Language and Language Disturbances,
Aphasic Symptom Complexes and Their Significance for Medicine and
Theory of Language* (New York, Grune and Stratton, 1948); and
Schutz's detailed study, *CP 1,* "Language, Language Disturbances and
the Texture of Consciousness," 260–86.

27. See the works cited above, nn. 12, 22, 24.

discussion of these various theories, we may sum up their
findings very briefly, selecting merely the features important
for our present problem.

1. There is no such thing as an isolated experience. Any
experience is experience within a context.[28] Any present experience receives its meaning from the sum total of past experiences which led to the present one and is also connected by
more or less empty anticipations to future experiences, the
occurrence of which may or may not fulfill these expectations.
The present experience was, in a certain sense, always anticipated and expected in the past—of course not as this particular,
unique experience, but in a typical way.[29]

It may happen, however, that the present experience turns
out to be partially or even completely different from (perhaps
even contradictory with) our previous expectations; in such
a case we should say that our typical anticipations were not
fulfilled but annihilated, "exploded," by what actually occurs.[30]
Even so, the meaning-context of the experience which does occur with the preceding anticipations is preserved: the new experience proves to be "against all expectations," "otherwise
than anticipated," "unforeseen." Yet precisely because there
is this deviation from what was foreseeable, the meaning-context includes both the previous expectations of the present
annihilation of these expectations. In this sense Leibniz could
state that the present is always the outcome of the past and the
past is pregnant with the future.

*The first meaning-context of any experience is therefore that
which connects it with the past experiences and the anticipated
future ones.* This context is of course based upon the auto-

28. Gurwitsch's study, *The Field of Consciousness,* is a detailed examination of this. It was not completed when Schutz wrote the present
study, but the two philosophers frequently discussed this and other issues
for many years.

29. Insofar as every lived-experience *(Erlebnis)* is "protentive" (and
also, of course, retentive), each includes automatic ("passive") "anticipations" of future phases of the same mental life. Cf. above, Ch. 1, n. 17;
and Husserl, *Ideen I,* Secs. 81–82.

30. Cf. Husserl, ibid., Secs. 105, 106, 138.

biographical situation of the experiencing mind, but it neverthe-less has its typical style whose features can be investigated and described without special reference to the autobiographical circumstances. One of these features is the double idealization which Husserl, speaking in terms of the experienced content, called "and so forth and so on," and in terms of the experienc-ing subject (whatever may be the specific activities or actions), "I can do it again."[31]

Such idealizations are but several of the constitutive factors of meaning-context we here have in view. In any event, it is clearly impossible, in these terms, to break down the unit of a meaning-context into elements which are unconnected with past experiences—at the very least with those which are just im-mediately past (i.e. those which are "still in one's grip," i.e. retention as opposed to recollection)—and with the anticipa-tions of immediately immanent occurrences (i.e. protentions as opposed to expectations of more distant occurrences). This, then, is the first explanation of the impossibility of atomizing our experiences into elements detached from the meaning-context just outlined.

2. We continually experience our own organism as a func-tional whole which is always within a concrete situation with which, as Goldstein puts it, it must "come to terms."[32] This phenomenon (i.e. the subjective experience of our functioning body as a unit) has been phenomenologically analyzed, espe-cially by the French existentialists Jean-Paul Sartre and Maurice Merleau-Ponty.[33] It is due merely to the clumsiness

31. See above, Ch. 2, n. 12.
32. See Kurt Goldstein, *The Organism: A Holistic Approach to Biology, Derived from Pathological Data in Man* (New York, American Book Company, 1939), esp. pp. 87–99, 213–90, 339 f.; also Gurwitsch, *Studies in Phenomenology and Psychology,* "Goldstein's Conception of Biological Science," pp. 69–88, and "Gelb-Goldstein's Concept of Concrete and Categorial Attitude and the Phenomenology of Ideation," pp. 359–84.
33. See Sartre, *L'Être et le néant,* pp. 368–430 (E. T., pp. 303–60); Merleau-Ponty, *Phénoménologie de la perception,* esp. Part I; and Zaner, *The Problem of Embodiment,* Parts II and III. Schutz has criti-cally reviewed Husserl's discussion of the animate organism in *CP 3,*

and vagueness of ordinary speech that one can say, "I am extending my hand in order to grasp this or that." *I am my hand*
which reaches for the glass of water, and *I am the mouth* to
which the hand raises the glass. *I am the eye* which perceives
the glass, and *I am the tongue* which tastes the coldness of the
liquid.[34]

Subjectively speaking, the act of drinking water is an unbreakable unity, an experience pertaining to my organism
which creates a meaning-context for all the manifest phases of
bodily actions and reactions involved. Only if an obstacle
occurs, if this ongoing unified process is interrupted for one
reason or another, does the unfinished part of the hitherto
unified action become isolated; standing out for itself, it becomes a particular problem to be solved.

Such "interruptions of tasks to be performed," so overestimated by current psychology (as in Zeigarnik's experiments), will be studied later.[35] The phenomenon has been
elucidated by the many cases of language disturbances studied
by Goldstein. Whereas the normal person, having no interruptions in the flux of his organic functions, uses language as a
simple means—i.e. as a habitual possession which he uses in
order to "come to terms" with his environment—the patient
suffering from certain organic difficulties loses the ordinary
meaning-context of his speech and its elements. He will become
distressed and undergo a catastrophic shock. He will nevertheless try to overcome this in such a way that his whole organism

---

"Edmund Husserl's Ideas, Volume II," 15–39 (see Husserl, *Ideen zu
einer reinen Phänomenologie und phänomenologischen Philosophie,*
Bk. 2: *Phänomenologische Untersuchungen zur Konstitution,* edited by
Marly Biemel, *Husserliana* Band IV [The Hague, Martinus Nijhoff,
1952]).

34. There is an important sense in which, despite the "unbreakable
unity" to which Schutz refers here, I am *not* my body. Cf. Zaner, "The
Radical Reality of the Human Body," *Humanitas, 2* (1966) 73–87.

35. See below, Ch. 5. For the reference to B. V. Zeigarnik, cf., e.g.,
The Pathology of Thinking (Consultants Bureau of New York, 1965),
esp. pp. 9–40 and 67–104. Although it is uncertain which work Schutz
had in mind, this one deals with the issues and has an excellent bibliography of Zeigarnik's work, pp. 198–99.

sets into play other means in order to come to terms with the situation newly created by the organic disturbances. In our terminology, the patient has to find new meaning-contexts in which the elements of his actions, which have lost their original meaning-context, can be functionally experienced as a unit.

We have already noted Goldstein's statement that the organism has "to come to terms with its environment." It would be a serious misunderstanding—but one which is common to much current psychology—to interpret this notion as a mere "adjustment to the environment." *Environment,* as will become clear later on, is not a sector of the world simply imposed upon us from the outside, something which we must take as not of our own making and with which we may come to terms only if we "adjust" or "adapt" ourselves to it. At best this is but an aspect of its meaning. The environment has as well its subjective aspect for the organism; it is the outcome and product of our selection of that sector of the world which we consider and acknowledge as relevant for the functioning of our activities— organic as well as mental—as a whole.

It is true that we are always "in situation," as Heidegger and the French existentialists say.[36] But it is up to us to "define this situation," as American sociologists, following W. I. Thomas, call it, and therewith the environment can no longer be conceived as being exclusively imposed on us. Rather, it becomes intrinsically relevant to the ongoing flux of our activities; it is, if not of our own making, nevertheless of our definition, and such "definition" is precisely the way in which we come to terms with it.

These remarks are merely anticipations of a more complete analysis of the problems covered by the term "environment"— analysis which becomes possible only after the investigation of

36. Man is not in the world like a pea in a pod, separable and removable without alteration; his being in the world (and in particular situations and circumstances therein) is a constitutive moment of his being as such. Cf. Sartre, *L'Être et le néant,* pp. 508–642 (E. T., pp. 433– 556); and Heidegger, *Sein und Zeit* (8th ed. Tübingen, Neomarius Verlag, 1957), pp. 52–112 *(Being and Time,* tr. John Marquarrie and Edward Robinson [New York, Harper & Row, 1962], pp. 78–148).

the biographically determined conditions of the world, those which remain taken for granted, has been accomplished. Our brief outline of Goldstein's concept of "coming to terms with the environment" and the disturbances of the ongoing, habitually possessed activities has, however, shown the importance of this interpretation—which is by no means restricted to organic language disturbances, but can be applied to nearly all forms of psychiatric disturbances of meaning-contexts established by the uninterrupted functioning of the organism (in respect of its being subjectively experienced as an indivisible whole).

The unit originating in the subjective experience of the functioning organism as a whole provides another explanation of the constitution of meaning-contexts which resists further analysis.

3. The unity of objects in the outer world, so far as our experiences of them are concerned, seems to originate in the objects themselves. Here the Gestalt psychologists have made great contributions to our modern conception of the hypothesis of constancy.[37] Things in the outer world have their own particular locations among other things which surround them; they stand out from a background of other things. They have their particular Gestalt, determined either by the continuity of their contour lines or by their regular or irregular distribution on a continuous ground in terms of which the missing contour lines are supplied by a habitual mental "filling-in" of the vacancies; the seemingly discontinuous elements are thus transformed into the continuity of contours supplied by such habitualities. The single objects, say the three points

are thus conceived—even apperceived—as terminals of a triangular contour, not in isolation but in the shape of the triangle of which they form the end points.

On the other hand, objects of the outer world have their

37. For the most penetrating discussion of the constancy hypothesis see Gurwitsch, *The Field of Consciousness,* pp. 51 ff., 90 ff., passim.

phases in outer time. When changing they have their "gliding phases" of transition—which are conceived as *Bewegungser-scheinungen,* studied especially by Wertheimer.[38] They have their "fore-and-aft" (in the sense of time-structure), but these changes are changes conceived and apperceived in the unity of a phase which forms a time Gestalt of its own and cannot be broken down into its single phases—at least not under normal conditions. The flying bird, the marching man, are observed in the unbreakable meaning-context of flying and marching. This is due to what Bergson called the cinematographic function of the mind.[39] And an artificial destruction of this meaning-context (for example, by the device of a snapshot by a camera, or a slow motion movement produced by the cinematographic technique) is required in order to break down the units of the meaning-context into elements, and this is not meaningful at all, or at least is meaningful only in a context other than that prevailing in our natural lifeworld.

Gestalt is therefore the habitual possession of meaning-contexts which supply the indivisible unit of the phenomenal configurations in which we apprehend the objects of the outer world.

4. Another form of the unit of a meaning-context might be found in the symbolic systems (in Ernst Cassirer's sense[40]) which serve as vehicles of our thinking.

To take language as an example, we find that any term in a proposition has a certain meaning first of all with respect to the total system of the vernacular to which it belongs (say, as a term

38. Cf. Max Wertheimer, "Untersuchungen zur Lehre von der Gestalt," Part I, *Psychologische Forschung, 1* (1921); Part II, *Psychologische Forschung, 4* (1923).

39. Cf. Bergson, *Les données immédiates de la conscience,* pp. 76–84, 170 f. (E. T., pp. 101–12, 227 f.); also *Creative Evolution* (New York, The Modern Library, 1944), Ch. 4.

40. Cf. Ernst Cassirer, *An Essay on Man* (New Haven, Yale University Press, 1944), esp. Part I; and his *Philosophy of Symbolic Forms* (3 vols. New Haven, Yale University Press, 1953, 1955, and 1957). See also Schutz's discussion of Cassirer, *CP 1,* "Language, Language Disturbances and the Texture of Consciousness," esp. 272 ff., and "Symbol, Reality and Society," esp. 289 f.

in the system of the English language currently in use in the United States). But it has its meaning within the particular sentence in which it is used, a meaning determined in part by the functional rules of the particular language (i.e. its grammar). And this is only half the story. As William James has already discovered,[41] every word has a conceptual *kernel* of meaning which it designates, that is, the meaning which can be found in dictionaries. This kernel is surrounded, however, by a "halo" or system of "fringes" of diverse sorts. There are, for instance, fringes of relations connecting this word in its particular meaning-context within a particular sentence in which it occurs with preceding and succeeding terms. Through these fringes, the word has its particular meaning within the structure not only of the isolated sentence but within the whole context of speech to which this sentence belongs.

There are other fringes relating to the particular situation in which the term is used, to the situations of the speaker and listener in the course of a conversation, to the whole past of the stream of meditation within which a term occurs in the thought of a thinker reflecting by himself, and so on. Beyond these, there are fringes resulting from previous uses of the term in particular circumstances, emotional fringes provoked not by the conceptual character of the term but by its evocative incantation, fringes of associations with words phonematically related, and the like.

This net of fringes surrounding the conceptual kernel of meaning cannot arbitrarily be destroyed without annihilating the meaning-context itself. To be sure, the isolated term still keeps the meaning of the conceptual kernel but the full functional meanings it has within the context of its fringes have been destroyed. We could go even further and consider that, for example, in the English language the breakdown of a word into its syllables—provided that no case of prefixes, suffixes, or inflectionary parts is involved—destroys even the meaningful kernel. But it is sufficient to think of the nonsensical word-

41. Cf. James, *Principles of Psychology, 1,* 281 f.

groups resulting from the juxtaposition of grammatically un-related terms (for instance, "king either however belonged") which Husserl studied in the fourth of his well-known *Logical Investigations,* devoted to the problem of a general grammar.[42] The same holds good for a group of mathematical symbols, each of which can keep its individual meaning but can become nonsensical by reason of the destruction of the meaning-context deriving from its functional context—such as $\sqrt{} + = x$.

On the other hand, ongoing ordinary speech has its natural articulations, its rhythmic patterns, even in prose, which permit us to stop at certain "resting points" and to produce, if not the full meaning context of a thought to be expressed, then at least a partial meaning, a meaning-fragment in itself. The outer tokens of these resting points in the flight of speech are, in the written language, the punctuation marks—which graphically represent the pulsations of inflectional speech. If artificial rest-ing points are created, if the stretches of flight are interrupted where there is no juncture, the meaning-context is willfully de-stroyed. It is not by mere chance, nor a misused metaphor, that we speak of *articulation in speech and thought.* Sentences may remain unfinished, elliptical, interrupted. If the interruption does not occur at a natural resting point, and if the missing link to the meaning-context is not supplied by the fringes con-necting the elliptic utterance with well-determined elements arising from the situation in which the discourse takes place, such an elliptic statement remains ununderstandable. On the other hand, an isolated word (for instance, an interjection) might have its full meaning-context, deriving from the fringes by which it is related to unequivocal elements of the situation.

It would be erroneous to believe that this particularity of linguistic articulation is due to the conceptual structure of speech. A musical theme, however simple or complicated, is as a whole a meaningful unit without any conceptual reference. It nevertheless has its articulations, its stretches of flight and its resting points, the correct determination of which the

42. Cf. Husserl, *Logische Untersuchungen, 2,* Part 1 (4th ed. Halle a.d.S., Max Niemeyer, 1928), pp. 294–345.

musician calls "phrasing." By means of this articulation, the
theme can be and for the most part is broken down into
meaningful subunits which as such can be recognized, and in
many musical forms it furnishes the material of the "development" of the theme. But one cannot break down the theme
into meaningful subunits by arbitrarily selecting simply any
group of successive notes of the theme. It can be broken down
only at the "modal points" provided by its immanent articulation.

The grammarian also knows and makes use of the term
"phrase." The dictionary defines it as a group of two or more
words, expressing a single idea but not forming a complete sentence. In speech as in music, the meaning-context (here called
the "idea") is destroyed if a phase is broken down into the
words (sounds) of which it is composed even if the single detached words keep their significance as meaningful kernels.

*What has been exemplified by speech and music is, however,
a general feature of mental life itself.* Whether or not it goes on
as an indiscernible, equally structured stream, it has its characteristic pulsation, its rhythm, by which the inner duration is
articulated. Although this is not the place to prove a statement
where the analysis would require investigations far beyond the
purpose of this study, we venture the hypothesis that it is the
tension of our consciousness (in Bergson's sense) which reg-
ulates the rhythm of this pulsation and articulation. Any level
of this tension, any finite province of meaning,[43] will therefore
show its particular rhythmization, its particular propulsion in
which the articulation of the stream of consciousness materializes. If the metaphorical use of a term common in physics
were not so dangerously open to misunderstanding, we might
find in this particular structure of the mind an analogy to the
quantum of energy as understood by modern physics.

5. A particular form of the constitution of a meaning-context which needs to be mentioned here in view of its interest for

43. Schutz refers here to his development of James' theory of "multiple realities"; cf. *CP 1*, "On Multiple Realities," and "Symbol, Reality
and Society," esp. 340–46.

us in a later part of this study likewise shows that while it is subdivisible into subunits it resists being treated atomistically. This is the unification of projected conduct, our action, by the span of the project itself.

We are not yet in possession of all the elements needed for a full analysis of this situation. But we may tentatively call attention to the fact that it is only the actor who can determine what the goal of his action is. His project defines the state of affairs he wishes to bring about by means of his action as its outcome and result, and it is this goal or end which establishes the meaning-context for all the phases in which his ongoing action materializes itself. Living in his action, he has only this projected goal or end in view, and for this very reason he experiences all of his acting as a meaningful unit.

This thesis explains another phenomenon worth mentioning here, namely, that of the articulation of our in-order-to motives into a hierarchy of the interdependent plans. It also sheds new light on the problem dealt with in Section C (the polythetic and monothetic grasping of experience). In fact, the main topics selected in this chapter for illuminating the genesis of the sedimentations of our experiences are more or less arbitrarily selected aspects of the same basic texture of our conscious life.

The problem concerning the basic unit of experiences, of the impossibility of breaking experience down into homogeneous elements, is of the greatest importance for the meaning-context under which our stock of knowledge at hand is grouped. This context is the sedimentation of the various factors determining the unit structure of our experience—whether we conceive the latter (a) in terms of the immanent time-structure of experience, (b) as the outcome of polythetic steps which are monothetically grasped, (c) as Gestalt configurations, (d) as the flying stretches and resting places of the pulsations of our consciousness, or (e) in the case of our projected conduct, as the unit originating in the project of our actions. In all circumstances these genetic features of the history of our knowledge are of decisive importance for the structurization of the world in which we live, known to us in our natural attitude sufficiently for our purposes at hand.

E. The Chronological Sequence of Sedimentation and the System of Relevance

But the formation of our stock of knowledge at hand has its history in another sense as well, namely, it is *autobiographical*. It is of the greatest importance to know in what chronological order and at which moments of our conscious life the single elements of our knowledge were acquired. If we assume for a moment two individuals having at a certain time exactly the same stocks of knowledge at hand—of course, an impossible assumption—this would not only involve that these two persons went through the same experiences, each one having lasted through the same amount of time and having been apperceived with the same degrees of intensity, but also that the sequence in which the single experiences occurred was exactly the same. Bergson has shown that all these postulates would have to be fulfilled in order to justify the proposition that Peter's and Paul's consciousnesses have the same content.[44] He has also shown that the question concerning the identity of content of Peter's and Paul's consciousnesses is meaningless—since if all the aforementioned prerequisites were fulfilled, the two consciousnesses would be identical, and thus Peter and Paul would be identically the same person.

The problem concerning the chronological sequence in which knowledge of the same topic supposedly on the same level of clarity, distinctness, and precision is required, is of course well known. It is the central problem involved in the techniques of teaching and learning. Any subject requires its particular form of approach and this form varies among the cultures and times, as any history of education clearly shows. To give just one example, it cannot be said[45] that the well-trained American lawyer is superior to the well-trained French lawyer or vice versa. Yet in civil law countries, the student of law is trained for several years in the system first of Roman

44. Cf. Bergson, *Les données immédiates de la conscience,* 139–42 (E. T., pp. 184–89).
45. Schutz marked the passage from here to the end of the paragraph for deletion.

law, then of the national law of his country, then in the techniques of application and interpretation of the law, and only in the last stage of his training does he study actual cases. The student in an American law school will start with case analysis and will from there arrive at an insight into the theory of law as such, of evidence, of interpretation, and so on.

On the other hand it would be erroneous to believe that any approach to a corpus of knowledge (say, to a particular science) has to start from the basic definitions determining its object and fundamental concepts and axioms and then proceed to build up *more geometrico* theorem by theorem, deduction on deduction. First, such a system of teaching and learning would fit merely deductive sciences and would not be applicable to empirical or inductive ones. Second, we have a series of well-advanced sciences which nevertheless cannot adequately define their subject matter. Biology cannot explain what life really is; medicine has no satisfactory definition of health and disease; many schools of thought conflict in their attempts to define the nature of law; the limits of economic action are more than controversial; much of modern psychology has banned the term and concept of "soul" from its field of concern; and Hilbert starts his famous axiomatic of geometry with the assumption that there exists a class of objects $\alpha, \beta, \gamma, \ldots$ called points, another class $a, b, c \ldots$ called lines, and so on. Axiomatization and precision regarding the fundamental concept of any science whatever belong to very late stages of its development.

We do not, however, have to turn to the rather highly rationalized forms of knowledge as incorporated in the body of scientific propositions believed to be valid at a certain time in order to understand the importance of the sequence in which the single elements of knowledge have been acquired. Piaget and his collaborators have shown in a series of monographs how slowly and gradually the child grasps concepts and situations connected with space, time, causality, mathematics, and the like.[46] He has indeed proved that it would be impossible to teach a child, for instance, problems relating to causality

46. Cf. Piaget, *The Origins of Intelligence in Children,* and *The Construction of Reality in the Child* (New York, Basic Books, 1954).

before his general mental development has attained a level at which the underlying basic concept makes sense to him. Untimely knowledge, even of matters of fact, may lead to serious disturbances, as the case studies of psychoanalytic writers amply show.

But even if we as adults look back at our own autobiographies, we will most certainly discover some decisive experiences which determined the course of our lives by the mere fact that they were had at a particular time under the constellation of circumstances then prevailing. Our lives took another turn than they might have because we read a book at a particular stage of our development, made the acquaintance of a person at a specific moment, suffered at this time from a disease, learned disappointment, poverty, or kindness too early or too late. All these experiences entered our stocks of knowledge at hand, but their sedimentation shows a particular *profile* due to the time of their occurrence (when and at what point of our development this knowledge was acquired).

This phenomenon of timing or chronological sequence, we believe, can be explained by the theory of relevances which we have been developing. The emergent topical relevance constitutes what is thematic in our experience as that which stands out from a horizon of surrounding things habitually known at this particular moment and therefore taken for granted without question until further notice. Once constituted, the topic becomes the determining factor for the establishment of a system of interpretational relevances of those elements of our knowledge to be pulled from the horizon into the kernel in order to ascertain the place of the topically relevant experience within the stock of knowledge at hand. Now, those elements of knowledge which then serve as what is interpretationally relevant are in turn merely the sedimentation of previous experiences which were at that time topically relevant.

It can now be seen that the more complete the set of elements of knowledge is which can be used as interpretationally relevant as regards an emergent topic, the less anonymous will be the type under which the topic is to be subsumed; hence, too, the greater are the chances of referring the topic to "familiar" aspects which are habitual possessions in the stock of knowledge at hand and are thus ready to become interpretationally relevant for the new topic. On the other hand, if at the time of the experience of topically relevant materials the elements relevant to its interpretation are not sufficiently complete (or "at hand"), then a new and perhaps somewhat distorted system of motivational relevances may emerge. The topic is then seen in an unfamiliar, strange perspective; it evokes nonhabitual anticipations and expectations, as a consequence of which we are more uncertain (or hopeful or fearful) in dealing with it because sufficient interpretational material is not at hand. We meet the object with a particularly focused interest—an exaggerated or unusually weak one. We are therefore motivated either to enter more deeply than we habitually do into the inner and outer horizons of this topic, or else to drop it, to cover it by other topical relevances and to turn to other, more gratifying tasks. When this occurs, we leave the topic in suspense as something unknown or unknowable, laden with hopes or fears; it is something which simply has to be accepted or believed, or as being of no concern. This happens especially if the topic in question was imposed upon us at a time when we were not prepared to deal adequately with it, due to a lack of sufficient interpretationally relevant information. The usual adult, thinking of the many experiences imposed on him during his youth, will say: "I was too young and inexperienced at this time to grasp the full importance of the event." Or he may in another instance regretfully state: "If I only had known in my youth what I know today!"

The phenomenon with which we are here concerned seems important in several respects. First, it explains another particular aspect of the impact of the genetic sedimentation on the structure of habitually possessed knowledge at hand. Second, it sheds new light on the interconnectedness among the three systems of relevances—especially the motivational relevance system which leads to an evaluation of things known as functionally dependent on the actual interest at hand. Third, it may possibly serve for or function in the typification of the personality structure, its typical successes and failures, and so on, explained by the biographical sequence of its experiences. It might be tentatively suggested that an analysis of Piaget's findings will corroborate this possibility. It is also possible that Kardiner's concept of basic personality,[47] so skillfully used for the understanding of primitive cultures, actually aims at the typification of the structural features of the stock of knowledge at hand, although certainly in a rather inadequate way.

47. Cf., e.g., Abram Kardiner, *The Individual and His Society: The Psychodynamics of Primitive Social Organization,* with Foreword and Two Ethnological Reports by Ralph Linton (New York, Columbia University Press, 1939), esp. pp. 109–34, 409–87.

Before proceeding to the structural analysis of the stock of knowledge, we must discuss a group of interconnected features in the genetic organization of the stock of knowledge at hand, features which influence the structure of the sedimented habitual possessions. As we have seen, what is topically relevant determines the depth or level of investigation required to solve the problem in an adequate manner. It thus determines how far we must enter into the inner or outer horizons of the topic and the extent to which interpretationally relevant material has to be brought into consideration. This process may be carried out unhampered until an adequate solution of the problem has been achieved. But, certain disturbances may occur to interrupt or inhibit it, in the following ways.

(a) The process might be interrupted for good at a certain stage—that is, without any intention of being resumed—and the attempt to solve it is dropped, either because it "disappears" before an adequate solution has been obtained, or because other problems turn up which overshadow it (and thus it is dropped as well). (b) The process might be only temporarily interrupted, in order to be taken up again later on. (c) It might be repeated, that is, the topical phenomenon may be believed to be sufficiently treated at one time but require reinterpretation later, and even to need a new solution. We must consider each of these more carefully.

1. This chapter was included in the original manuscript as Section F of the previous chapter. However, due to its length and its unitary content, it was decided to make it into a separate chapter.

A. Disappearance of the Topic

In the first case, the topic is dropped without any intention of being reactivated. It is released from grip, or has lost its topical relevance; it is thus not a problem any more, either because (1) it has "ceased to exist," or (2) it has been merely overshadowed or covered over by newly emergent topics. Both situations may occur either intrinsically or by being imposed on us. We cannot enter into the full analysis of the casuistic involved here, but restrict ourselves to giving some significant examples.

1. One of the main cases in which the topic disappears completely is when we leap from one level or province of reality (or meaning) to another. As will be explained in the last part of this study,[2] we live simultaneously on different levels of reality (provinces of meaning), which are determined by the tension of consciousness, the degree of our awakeness, or, in other words, of our attention to life.[3] So to speak, we bestow the accent of reality on one or another level of our conscious life. Changes in level occur through a specific and basic experience, which might be characterized objectively as a "leap" and subjectively as a "shock."

One such level is that of the world of daily life, in which we are "wide-awake" and immersed in our tasks and chores, working among fellowmen, performing actions which gear into the world, changing and modifying it in numerous ways. This level is that of paramount reality, the home base and starting point of our existence.[4] All other levels or provinces might be interpreted as modifications of or derivations from paramount reality. There are also, however, the many differently structured worlds of phantasy, from our daydreams to the various worlds of fiction (as when we are immersed in the reality of works of art). There are also the worlds or provinces of play, of jokes,

2. Not included in the present study.
3. See above, Ch. 4, n. 43.
4. Concerning the reasons for designating the world of wide-awake, everyday living as "paramount," see CP 1, "On Multiple Realities," esp. 226 ff., and "Symbol, Reality and Society," esp. 341 ff.

of the mentally disturbed, of theoretical contemplation, and of our dreams.

While living in any of these worlds (on which we then bestow the "accent of reality"), we live in the various systems of relevances peculiar to it. There are, that is, topical, motivational, and interpretational relevances pertaining to the world of dreams, of play, of theory, and so on. If we "leap" from one level to another, we leave behind all the systems of relevances operative merely within its limits. The topic of a dream, for instance, is vitally important while the dream lasts; it creates the agony of a nightmare because we were unable to solve the problem involved. It loses its topical relevance through the experience of shock involved in shifting the level of reality—an experience we call "awakening." Of course, if fully awake we may think of this past topical relevance as "the dream I had last night"—but doing this means that we no longer hold in our grip what was experienced as topically relevant during the dream. We are not then dreaming anymore, but only thinking about experiences peculiar to another level of reality (although now in terms of systems of relevance belonging to the new level to which we have leaped). The case of the dream is so interesting that it deserves a brief analysis.

In remembering a dream, I am no longer dreaming; I have returned to the paramount reality of daily life. The topic of my dream, let us say, is still present to my mind, and I remember also that this topic was of particular relevance to me while I dreamed. It is not now relevant within the system of relevances prevailing in the reality of my wide-awake life. But I may nevertheless interpret the dream; but in doing so, I do not use the material defined by the system of interpretational relevances pertaining to my dream world. While dreaming, the dream-topic had its kernel, its particular inner and outer horizons, and it was from the latter that interpretationally relevant material was brought into the thematic dream-kernel. While I dreamed, I was guided by a system of in-order-to and because relevances prevailing exclusively within the dream world; my vital interest within the dream required that I find my way out of the magic spell which barred me from running after the person in whose hands (I was certain, while dreaming) was kept the secret of my existence. Now fully awake, I may well ponder the meaning of this dream, but insofar as I have this purpose I am no longer using the interpretational system of relevances which prevailed during my dream (while it was given the "accent of reality"), but rather the scheme of interpretational relevances considered as valid within the paramount reality of my daily life. In the same way, I no longer make use of the system of motivational relevances which rule my in-order-to and because motives within the dream world; those which prevail in, and are restricted to, the reality of my fully awake life are substituted.

Paradoxically, the main topic of my dream has disappeared by the sheer fact of my awakening; it was dropped entirely, released from my grip. In this now prevailing reality of wide-awake life, there is no one I must pursue in order to claim the secrets of my existence; consequently, there is no "reason," no valid motive for me, to attempt to pursue, and no experience of frustration because, in spite of all my efforts, I cannot move. If such a situation occurred within the reality of daily life, I could run after the person, capture him, reclaim what is mine. But in interpreting the dream, the tension, the irreconcilability of the system of relevances prevailing in the world of daily life with, and their irreducibility to, those prevailing in the world of the dream—these create a kind of substitute for the topical relevance for the dream, which has been truly dropped and annihilated. The topic disappeared, it left a vacancy; but since all interpretational and motivational relevances borrowed from the world of my wide-awake living refer to this absent topic, the vacancy which results from the missing link, from the dropped topic, becomes a kind of enclave within the reality of my daily life. It keeps its topical relevance, but now in a transformed setting of relevances; it is no longer genuinely topically relevant (as it was while I dreamed), but only in a derived and transformed sense. The vacancy is filled in with a new topic, a substitute which belongs to both worlds: to that of the dream, because the vacancy created by dropping the dream-topic still refers to the reality of the dream world left behind by my awakening; and to the world of daily life, because all interpretational and motivational relevances attached to this vacancy belong to this paramount reality, the vacancy being created by the dropping of a genuine topic on another level of reality and which vacancy I therefore call a *symbol*.

A symbol in this sense is thus an enclave in the actual level of reality resulting from the annihilation of a topically relevant theme of experiences originating on another level of reality. This at least is *one* among many other origins of symbolic transformation of reality[5] and the explanation of *one* of the many meanings with which the term symbol is fraught. It is, however, certainly the case that it is precisely that meaning which has been used in dream interpretations from the times of magical rituals—Pharao's dreams as interpreted by Joseph—up to the technique of modern psychoanalysis.

Our analysis of the dream is, of course, only an example of the various and manifold consequences in the genetic structure of our stock of knowledge at hand resulting from *the dropping of a topic on one level of reality and reinterpreting the vacancy created by this annihilation by means of systems of relevances belonging to other levels of reality.* "What is Hecuba to the actor?" asks Hamlet. What is Hamlet to us? Why are we deeply moved by participating in the destiny of the fictitious persons of a tragedy? Why do we gain a new kind of knowledge after having dwelt in the fictitious reality of a great work of art? How is it possible that religious experience reveals as a kind of knowledge, the truth of which cannot be grasped by the scheme of interpretational relevances prevailing in the world

5. Cf. Cassirer, *Language and Myth* (New York, Harper & Bros., 1946); and Suzanne Langer, *Philosophy in a New Key* (Cambridge, Harvard University Press, 1942). These philosophers along with Husserl, Bergson, and G. H. Mead, figure prominently in Schutz's discussion of symbols. Cf. *CP 1,* "Symbol, Reality and Society," esp. 287–92.

of daily life? All these many questions can be interpreted in terms of the shifting of systems of relevances prevailing on various levels of reality, a shifting which basically refers to the "loss" of the main topic prevailing at the level of reality left behind.

The change in levels may be an *imposed or an intrinsic one*. It is imposed upon me in the case of awakening from a dream. It is intrinsic to my plan of life, on the other hand, to leave the chores connected with my world of working for my leisure hours, to immerse myself for a time in the fictional world of a novel, to close the book whenever I please and return to the reality of my daily lifeworld. The distinction between imposed and intrinsic relevances is quite important also in other cases of change.[6]

We must now turn to examples of this phenomenon which do not involve a change in levels of reality. While writing in my study, I concentrate upon the topic of my task. Suddenly an unusual sound from the street interrupts the ongoing course of my activity. I get up in order to have a look through the window. Was it an explosion? A gunshot? Everything is quiet in the street and I come to the conclusion that "nothing extraordinary," nothing "deserving my attention," has happened. I return to my desk and take up my interrupted literary work.

I have dropped the topical relevance (namely, to discover the reason and source of the sound) for good without solving the problem involved. Only if the source were an explosion, a gunshot, or some other event (possibly dangerous or simply interesting), would it have been topically relevant—and thus worth my attention only so long as there was the open possibility that the origin and nature of the event was something like an explosion or a gunshot. Having ascertained that neither of these was the ground for my perception of this unusual sound, I am no longer interested in ascertaining whether it was caused by the backfire of an automobile or some other such event. The true reason for the sound is of no concern to me and the ex-

6. Schutz placed three "x's" in the margin next to this paragraph, possibly indicating a need to expand the analysis.

perience has lost its topical relevance. I drop it for good and release it from my grip.

In such a case the dropped topical relevance has *not* left an enclave, a vacancy which has to be reinterpreted in accordance with still subsisting systems of interpretational relevances and then filled in with a symbol. What actually occurred was that the event was only *hypothetically relevant*. My habitual possession is the knowledge that explosions or gunshots are typically important events requiring one of a number of courses of action—such as running away, looking for cover, aiding endangered people, and the like. When I heard the sound, this habitual possession created a system of motivational relevances, neutralized but ready to be reactivated at any time if circumstances imposed the transformation of neutrality into actuality. This is exactly the same kind of case as that we studied earlier, namely my fear of snakes. The explosionlike sound awoke the neutralized habitual possession of motivational relevances and created a hypothetically topical relevance: a topical *"relevance provided* that . . ." Having ascertained that the prerequisites for making the event topically relevant are not present, I come to the conclusion that the event is not topically relevant at all, strictly speaking, that it never was of any topical relevance but was merely erroneously believed to be of such a nature.

This is obviously a very simple example; but the same type of hypothetically relevant topics govern a great part of our actions in the natural attitude of daily life. They are brought on by our anticipations and expectations of future events and developments. We have "to watch" what happens because if events take this or that anticipated turn, the present state of affairs may become of highest importance. If what is anticipated does not occur, the present state of affairs is of no importance. It is then irrelevant and immaterial. In this way a series of topical relevances *"provided* that . . ." is created.

Yet here a very complicated *time structure* is involved. In anticipating a future turn of events at the present time, I am concerned with empty expectations which will or will not be fulfilled by the actually occurring events. Any topical relevance "provided that . . ." is therefore truly topically relevant *for the time being*—that is, as long as it cannot be ascertained whether the prerequisites of its topicality will or will not be fulfilled later on. This, however, remains entirely open at the present moment, although I may hope for or fear such fulfillment. In establishing a hypothetically topical relevance, I just imagine that an event of a certain type and nature *will have taken place;* I place myself at a point in the future, seen from which the actual situation *will* turn out retrospectively *to have been* relevant. This way of thinking shall be called thinking in the future past tense—the *modo futuri exacti.*[7]

On the other hand, there are cases where a present state of affairs seems to be possibly topically relevant because I know from previous experiences that there is typically a chance that typical situations like the present one may take the anticipated turn. We usually call such a topical relevance "provided that . . ." the *significative relevance,*[8] and we say that the present state of affairs is a *sign* for the emptily anticipated possible turn of affairs which, if fulfilled, would prove to be the genuine topical relevance of my actual experience. If not fulfilled, my expectations will "explode," the hopes attached to them will be frustrated or the fears connected with them will turn out to have been without foundation—as when I say that I overestimated the importance of the event, or overweighed its significance, or I saw things in the wrong perspective and thus thought I found signs where really none could be found.

What has been said concerning one important aspect of symbols holds good for the present discussion of sign and significance: it is only *one* aspect, one among many of the connotations of the term "sign," that can be explained by the theory of topical relevances "provided that . . ." which we interpreted

7. For further analysis of this phenomenon, see *PSW,* pp. 57–63; and *CP 1,* "Choosing Among Projects of Action," esp. 68 f., and "On Multiple Realities," esp. 214–18.

8. Schutz marked this term as unsatisfactory without, however, indicating the reason for this.

in terms of the *modo futuri exacti* mode of thinking.[9] It is, however, what we commonly understand by the term, as when we say that a particular formation on the surface of the earth is a sign for the geologist to find oil at a certain depth, that a halo around the moon is a sign of rain the other day, and so on.

Hypothetically topical relevances will become of special importance when we later turn to the detailed analysis of projected human conduct, which we call action.[10] The project of such conduct anticipates in phantasy, by way of a sort of mental rehearsal, as Dewey puts it,[11] the as yet unperformed action, imagining it as having been accomplished in the future past tense.

2. Another aspect of the relationship between project and action leads us to the second subdivision of the disappearance of topical relevances, namely the case in which the original topical relevance is dropped because another problem turns up —one which is connected with the first in such a way that it is covered by and hidden behind the new topic. The typical case is the following one: a certain course of action has been projected in order to attain a certain goal by a chain of means to be put into play. In implementing this project by designing in detail the single steps to be carried out or the means to be brought successively within reach, it turns out that the last step, the end of the contemplated chain of actions, has lost its topical importance. This occurs because it either proves to be only an intermediate one within a wider project, or because some of the steps leading to the realization of the originally conceived project are not practicable, that is they cannot be translated into the reality of the world of working—either be-

9. Schutz marked this sentence unsatisfactory. He also felt that the following examples were questionable.

10. See above, Ch. 1, n. 9.

11. Cf. John Dewey, *Human Nature and Conduct* (New York, Henry Holt Co., 1922), Part III, Sec. III: "The Nature of Deliberation." In deliberation, Dewey says, "each conflicting habit and impulse takes its turn in projecting itself upon the screen of imagination. It unrolls a picture of its future history, of the career it would have if it were given head." (p. 190)

cause the means of attaining it cannot be brought as supposed within reach, or they can be brought within reach but they lead to unexpected secondary consequences inconsistent with the original project.[12]

In both cases (that of the extended and that of the restricted course of action) we say that the newly established project in its topical relevance covers or hides the original genuine project. The latter is absorbed by the former and is no longer in view; its topical relevance is superseded by that of the newly emergent project. Retrospectively, it may seem that the situation was exactly the inverse, that is that the new project was hidden by the implication of the original one, and only came into view when the old one was dropped. This situation frequently occurs if the system of originally intrinsic relevances cannot be established without interruption, that is if it becomes disturbed by another system of relevances (such as one not of our own making but imposed on us). It is not difficult to find examples of this kind of occurrence, especially when we turn to the history of discoveries and inventions as well as the history of the sciences. Alchemists who attempted to transform ordinary minerals into gold made most important metallurgical discoveries; Columbus sought a new route to India and discovered a new world; a discussion of the axioms of geometry furnishes a new tool for the general theory of relativity and thus provided a mathematical explanation of a curved, closed, and infinite universe.

But more generally, anyone who tries to write down a well-conceived train of thought (be it merely a simple letter to a stranger or to a business firm) will find that in the course of his writing, articulating, and elaborating his thought, new topical relevances come up, with the result that the finished product is necessarily other than the projected one. It is a general principle of the theory of action that the act, once performed, turns

12. Schutz added the following marginal note to this sentence: "Es können sich auch die 'Mittel' zu Selbstzwecken verselbständigen—ein Fall für soziologische Theorie." ("It could also make the 'means' themselves independent—a case for sociological theory."

out to be different from the action just projected: "Ein anderes Antlitz, eh sie geschehen, ein anderes zeigt die vollbrachte Tat."[13] The reason for this will be explained at the appropriate place; here we are concerned especially with the phenomenon of *covering*, of the disappearance of the former topical relevances behind the newly emergent ones.

The phenomenon in question will become of particular importance for the theory of social action, which is characterized by the fact that to the actor, the other's (my fellowman's) intrinsic relevances are imposed, they delimit the freedom of displaying and following up his own system of intrinsic relevances. Thus, for instance, a chessplayer has to modify his projected course of action with each move his partner makes. A general must adjust his tactical and strategical plans to the measures taken by his opponent; the businessman has to adjust his policy in accordance with the behavior of his competitors, clients, and so on. In any case, there is an element of surprise inherent to the newly emergent and unanticipated relevances which supersede and cover the former set. Merton has applied the term "serendipidity"[14] to this phenomenon. It originates in the fact that all of our anticipations are necessarily empty unless fulfilled or annihilated by the subsequent events. But this aspect of the problem refers to the logic of the unknown and the theory of aporetics which will be studied in the following part.[15]

B. The Process Temporarily Interrupted

We turn now to the study of the next group of disturbances affecting the sedimentation of our experiences, in which this process is temporarily interrupted while the intention to reassume the interrupted process persists. In such cases the topic

13. "One face before it happens, another after the fact."

14. Cf. Robert K. Merton, *Social Theory and Social Structure* (Glencoe, Free Press, 1949), pp. 12, 98–102, 375 ff. Merton writes, e.g., that serendipity, as he uses the term, is "the discovery through chance by a theoretically prepared mind of valid findings which were not sought for." (p. 12) Schutz obviously wants to broaden the usage.

15. Not included in the present study.

is not dropped, nor released from our grip for good, but merely neutralized; it is inactive but ready to be activated at any time when circumstances permit.

1. The interruption might be imposed or voluntary. In the first, it might be imposed by our very nature, or by the nature of things. Thus, for instance, our nature does not permit us to carry on certain of our activities through to their completion in one single stretch. Our consciousness shows a particular rhythm of various tensions: periods of full-awakeness are necessarily interrupted by periods of sleep, effort leads to fatigue, attention has its degrees of intensity. This rhythm of our inner life—and although having its biological-organic foundation, this rhythm is itself experienced subjectively as an occurrence of our inner life—articulates the rhythms of our activities requiring for their completion a period of time greater than that determined by this oscillation in the tension of our consciousness.

The interruption may be imposed by the nature of things: that is, if the development needed by the occurrences in outer time is beyond our control and not of our making, the particular phenomenon of "waiting" occurs. Waiting and fatigue are categories relating to the ontological situation of man within the world (and because they are fundamental relevances founded in the circumstances as determined by autobiographical factors, these phenomena shall be studied later on in the autobiographical setting).[16] Here we are merely concerned with the fact that these imposed interruptions lead to pauses, to intermissions, in our activities—which, of course, need not be imposed. They may originate in voluntary interruptions, as when we turn away from our topic and later revert to it. In both cases, the imposed and the voluntary, the problem arises: *What happened to the topic during the intermission?* How is it possible to revert to it after such a pause? Why can I expect to start tomorrow where I ended today? And have these questions to be answered in the same manner for imposed and for voluntary interruptions?

16. See below, Ch. 7.

Suppose I am reading *Don Quixote* and am interrupted; the answers to such questions seem relatively simple. I cannot finish the reading of the novel in one session; but closing the book tonight with Chapter Twenty, I may anticipate that tomorrow Chapter Twenty-one will give me the continuation of the story. Even if I do not continue until next week, or next month, I can be assured of starting where I left off today. Meanwhile, I may or must turn to other activities, other topics will be in the foreground of my concern, other relevances will emerge from the theme to which I attend during the intermission in my reading of the novel. Being neither a philologist nor a professional student of literature, my reading of this novel is reserved for my leisure time. I have, as we mentioned before, plans of various kinds integrating my various motives—plans of work and for leisure, for the hour and for the day, all of them organized in a hierarchy dependent upon my plan of life. These plans determine the motivational relevances of my activities. And therewith, the topical relevances founded upon such motives are determined. Within my plan for my leisure time, the topical relevance of continuing my reading subsists unchanged. It does not fit into my plan for work; and while working, it is neutralized, put in brackets, inactive, dormant but nevertheless still in my grip. It is, in short, a topic belonging to another system of plans, to another province of my life; the predominant topic of my leisure time is suspended but persists in neutralized form, ready to be reactivated. Of course, while occupied during my leisure time with the reading of the book, the topics belonging to my plan for work are left in abeyance, to be reinstated with the next turning to other systems of in-order-to motives, called my plans.

This example may lead to a misunderstanding, since the activities of my daily life pertain to the sphere of the paramount reality of working in the common world, whereas my reading of a novel requires my immersion in the reality of the world of fiction. To be sure, many of the so-called interruptions of the process of sedimentation of our experience will involve a change in the level of reality or province; and since we define the paramount reality of daily life as the world of full-awakeness founded upon full attention to life (which is the highest tension of consciousness), it is possible to explain even fatigue as a modification of such tension, and thereby of the paramount reality itself. But such a change in level of reality is not always involved in cases of intermission. Pauses and interruptions may occur, in other words, if systems of in-order-to motives belonging to the same level of reality intersect or compete. This happens in the example we are using.

If we interrupt our ongoing activity a_1 and turn to the activity a_2, reverting to a_1, after having finished a_2, we replace the theme a_1 and the topical relevances attached thereto by the theme a_2 and its topical relevances. a_2, thus far in the margin of the field of consciousness, is now brought into focus, while a_1 is relegated to the margin. But it is so relegated as a neutralized topic with all its attendant relevances: it is put off, deferred in its full topical relevance, but not released from my grip. Having a_2 in the center of my thematic field, with its full topical relevance, I nevertheless have a_1, in the margin as a topic in its own right, but now as a temporarily suspended one, a topic put in brackets but carrying along its full relevance structure in an inactive, neutralized mode. We may call such a topic "marginal," and the relevances attached to it "marginal relevances." Insofar as the latter are motivational relevances, we may even speak of marginal plans.

The difference between this situation and the two cases already dealt with is obvious.[17] In the first the topic has been dropped for good, it is no longer in the field of consciousness, not even in the margin. It may have left a vacancy, but the systems of relevances attached to this vacancy are not the relevances attached to the original topic (now released from our grip) but relevances related to the actual topic now in focus. In the second, where a topic is dropped in the sense of being "covered" by another one, it was essential that the newly emergent problem was connected with the first in such a way that the

17. Schutz is referring to the "dropping" of a topic (above, pp. 103–11) and to the "covering" of it (above, pp. 111–13).

former either extended or restricted the span of the latter. But in our present case (that of an interrupted, postponed activity) the deferred topic is kept in marginal grip; there is no vacancy which could serve as the origin of a system of heterogeneous relevances, and the marginal topic is not connected with the actual one by way of superposition. Marginal and actual topics compete with one another equally and with their full systems of relevance (the first, to be sure, in neutralized modification).

2. Accordingly, the full set of motivational relevances (which we call a plan) not actually in operation can be interpreted as a marginal topic. In this capacity it is deemed able to be put into operation again at any time at will, and if circumstances permit. Yet, strictly speaking, the assumption that I may start again tomorrow where I left off today involves an *idealization* which is a particular form of that called the "and so on and so forth," or the "I can do it again" mentioned earlier.[18] As a matter of fact, I cannot reassume the interrupted activity a_1 exactly where I shifted it from the focus to the margin of my field. During the pause, the intermission, it was a marginal topic and received by this very fact a particular tinge from the relevance systems pertaining to the then actualized topic a_2. My reassumed activity a_1 may be substantially the "same" as it was before the interruption, but it will always have the meaning of *"the same activity but continued after interruption."* It may be, of course, that this change of meaning has no other reason than that the course of protentions— that is, of anticipations of immediately impending occurrences in the flux of the uninterrupted realization of the ongoing activity—was interrupted by the intersecting new topic. The subjective corollary of this experience is the lesser or greater effort it takes to "get oneself going" after the intermission. This resumption of an interrupted activity is a special case of the *general problem of recurrence* which will become of particular importance for our study of certain forms of social interaction and social relationships.

18. See above, Ch. 2, n. 12.

We should recall, however, that our interrupting a_1 and taking up a_2 is either imposed on us or is the result of a voluntary shifting of our attentional focus. In the latter case this shifting is *motivated;* the experiencing of the shifting itself may become of topical relevance, but the latter is based upon motivational relevances of a particular kind. We could even introduce here a fourth category of relevance which might properly be called the *relevance of actualization.*

However, closer examination reveals that this relevance of actualization can be analyzed into several factors. (a) The motivational relevances of shifting from one activity to the other themselves belong to the general plan of life, within which all other plans—for work and leisure, for the hour and for the day, etc.—have their hierarchical position. *Relevance of actualization is therefore merely a system of motivational relevance of a higher order.* (b) The relevance of actualization may be referred to the ontological structure of our being in the world as mortal, having to husband our limited supply of time and energy. As a matter of fact, this problem will have to be studied again when we turn to the analysis of the biographical moments determining our situation with the world of circumstances. (c) In this same context, the limits imposed upon us by the ontological order of things in nature, including the biological requirements of our own organism, impose upon us an order of simultaneity and succession, that is of forms of intersection of events in outer time with our inner duration. The limitation imposed by simultaneity bars us from executing an infinite number of activities or experiencing an infinite number of things concomitantly. The order of succession creates an order of priorities and prerequisites within the situational circumstances, if not in terms of valuation, then in terms of chronology, which makes us do "first things first." (d) The relevance of actualization is founded, finally, on the fact that we live from the outset in a social world, that our knowledge is socially distributed and for the most part socially derived, and that the reconciliation of our own system of topical, interpretational, and motivational relevances with that of our fellowmen must needs remain a partial and fragmentary one.[19] By means of this overlapping of the individual systems of relevance, a new motive for actualization arises, the intrinsic relevances of my fellowmen being experienced by me as imposed relevances.

Here another distinction between imposed and voluntary interruption becomes visible: the imposed interruption—be it imposed by our human condition, by the nature of things, or by social intercourse—is subjectively experienced as an obstacle hindering the unhampered flux of our activities. The so-called voluntary interruption is also motivated by the same factors, but these motives, being genuine because motives, are merely revealed in the reflective attitude. Of course, interruption might be experienced as painful, may lead even to psychopathological phenomena. *But to a great extent the shifting from one activity to another, the interpenetration of our plans,* the chain of reciprocal interruption which dominates and articulates our whole life (bestowing on it a unique and individual rhythmical pattern), *becomes habitualized and as such a possession integrated into our stock of knowledge at hand, taken for granted without question.*

3. Modern psychology has become especially interested in the problem of interruption of tasks to be performed, and several ingenious experiments have been devised to show the influence of such artificial interruption on the efficiency of performing the interrupted tasks (Zeigarnik, Osianka).[20] We are not interested in the particular psychological problem involved here, especially since the laboratory situation has to do exclusively with imposed tasks and imposed interruptions, without making it clear what interruption itself means and when a task has to be considered as accomplished—not from the point of view of the observer (the psychologist) but of the acting subject.

19. For a more detailed analysis of this, see *CP 1,* "Symbol, Reality and Society," esp. 347–52; and *CP 3,* "Some Structures of the Lifeworld," pp. 116–32.
20. For the work of B. V. Zeigarnik, see above, Ch. 4, n. 35 (esp. the bibliography cited).

We are interested in the problem of interruption, rather, in several other respects. First, as we mentioned in our introductory remarks,[21] we have to be careful not to be misled by the necessarily static description of this genetic process into interpreting the relegation of the interrupted topic into the margin and the resumption of it as experiences which necessarily stand out in the ongoing flux of our conscious life segregated from all other experiences. Actual and marginal topics are copresent to our mind; they are simultaneous. We called this capacity of our mind to hold both of them in grip the "counterpointal structure of our mind," in virtue of which we are able to pursue, like the listener of a piece of polyphonic music, two independent themes simultaneously going on in the same flux, taking one as the focal center and the other as marginal, and vice versa. Second, we mentioned at the same place that this phenomenon is merely the corollary to what we called the schizophrenic-ego hypothesis, namely the fact that we are involved in the one actual and the many marginal topical relevances with layers of our personality on different levels of depth. This feature will become especially important for our further study. It is the starting point for the analysis of the concept of social role and social personality. Third, the interruption of the process of sedimentation of our knowledge, that is, the rhythmical oscillating between actual and marginal relevances, becomes of fundamental importance for the structure of our stock of knowledge at hand. This must be briefly explained.

If a permanent organization of mental life on various levels or depths occurs in such a manner that the mental activities are subsumed under systems of alternating actual and marginal relevances, then certain habitual possessions of knowledge emerge. Not only does the movement from one to another level become a matter of course (done without question), but as well the system of relevances particular to each set of activities becomes a habitual possession of unquestioned, taken for granted knowledge—unquestioned, however, only within the frame of this particular system of relevances. While set a_2 is actualized

21. Cf. above, pp. 11–13.

and set a_1 is still marginally in grip, the systems of relevances pertaining to a_1 as well as those belonging to a_2 may be habitually possessed and taken for granted without question. Yet, taking a_2 as the point of departure, as home base and point of reference, the relevance system attached to a_1 might become questionable, no longer taken for granted but problematic, and vice versa. The relevance system a_1 may appear consistent in itself but inconsistent with respect to the relevance system of a_2; what is a self-explanatory routine with a_1 may be incompatible with a_2 (although the rhythmical shifting from a_1 to a_2 and back might have become a matter of mere routine). If such a situation occurs—as it does, by necessity, because it originates in the counterpointal structure of the mind and the schizophrenic involvement of different depth-levels of our personality in either set of relevances—then the universal applicability of our stock of knowledge at hand breaks asunder. The stock of knowledge by means of which one masters problems of work are of no use in our leisure life. The businessman playing with his child "forgets about" business. The tension of consciousness has changed; popular language is perfectly accurate in speaking about hours of relaxation. In this sense, the intermission or pause is a disturbance of the unhampered process of sedimentation of knowledge. Yet, this unhampered sedimentation is only an idealized model, and the various phenomena we have handled thus far under the heading of deviation and disturbance of the process are rather the "normal" course of affairs.

C. Recommencing the Process

We have just studied the cases in which the topic was definitely released from grip without having reached a solution to the problem involved, and that in which the process of sedimentation was interrupted although the intention to reassume it remained. We must now turn to the case in which an adequate solution to the problem in question is believed to have been reached. The topic is assumed to have been delimited adequately for the purposes at hand and the process of sedimentation has come to a standstill, i.e. adequate knowledge of the topical problem has been obtained. But later on it turns out that the solution of the problem, the interpretation of the topic, was merely an incomplete one and that the whole process now has to be started again.

1. What was stored away as being adequately known, as no longer questionable, reveals unknown aspects of strangeness or implications in the as yet unexplored horizons inconsistent with what we believed to be sufficiently ascertained. Or, the meaning-context within which this object of our experience seemed to be sufficiently familiar is modified in some way or other: it is expanded or contracted, crossed by other meaning-contexts, varied in its immanent structurization; it has lost its specific character of habitual possession by superimposition of newly emergent topical relevances, and so on. In all these cases, new problems arise, affairs believed to be unquestioned and even beyond question (because immaterial and irrelevant as regards the original topic then at hand) become problematic and have to be explored. Yet these newly emergent questions cannot be answered in isolation, the new topical relevance cannot be detached from previously acquired knowledge of the supposedly same object and cannot be treated in isolation.

The latter is indeed characteristic for what distinguishes the present case from those discussed before. It is not simply an interruption of the process of sedimentation (occurring under the idealization "and so forth and so on," which involves the possibility of restarting and continuing today where I left off, or was interrupted, yesterday). Rather, the newly emergent or supervening topic requires a *radical recommencement of the whole process,* a revision of habitual possessions which are deprived of their character of sufficient ascertainment: we cannot now merely accept what we already know, or continue to take for granted what we have assured through previous processes. In fact, of course, it was taken for granted as a habitual possession merely "until further notice," and the supervening, emergent topical relevance is precisely this "further notice" which prevents us from abiding by the results achieved thus far. In this way, our habitually possessed knowledge of this particular topic, our familiarity with it, loses its character of habituality. We are no longer entitled to expect things to go on "and so forth and so on" as we habitually did thus far—and this cutting off of our anticipations itself becomes motivationally relevant for a radical reexamination of the topic involved.

Such a situation may occur because our previous anticipations "exploded," were annihilated by supervening experiences of newly emergent events. It may also occur by intrinsic shifts of our focal interest to material previously in the horizon which proves to be inconsistent with the system of interpretational relevances heretofore attached to the topical kernel, as determined by breaking off further investigation. Similarly, the situation in question may occur by means of newly imposed relevances (topical, interpretational, or motivational) imposed on us by the nature of things, our autobiographical situation, or, very frequently, by our fellowmen. Any combination of these factors, of course, is possible.

Moreover, it may be that the revision of habitualities and of dissolving the sedimentation underlying it refers either to a relatively well-circumscribed sector of our stock of knowledge at hand or to the factors determining its structurization as a whole—that is, to our typical way of forming systems of topical, interpretational, and motivational relevances which themselves belong to our stock of habitually possessed knowledge at hand. An example of the latter might be the need to regroup our system of in-order-to motives as a whole, namely our plan of life. If such a situation occurs—by imposition or intrinsically —then a turning point in our entire life has been reached which is commonly called a crisis. The principles of our habitual possessions become then questionable and our belief in the world as taken for granted breaks asunder.

But here we are concerned with the revision of more or less well-delimited sectors of our knowledge. All questions arise on the basis of what is not in question or even questionable, that is, our habitually possessed experiences which we take for granted without question. The problematic emerges on the foundation of the unproblematic, and the unknown refers to the familiar; the novel experience is novel because it cannot be related and referred to the sum total of known things. Yet, as we have seen, familiarity is such only as regards the typical, and the unexplored horizonal material is left unknown with respect to all the atypical aspects—which may turn out to be strange. All knowledge beyond question remains unquestioned because what we call known is so only in terms of its adequacy for the theoretical and practical purposes then at hand. Consequently, any kind of knowledge is determined by the level at which we break off further investigation as immaterial and irrelevant for such purposes at hand. By a voluntary fiat we declare our curiosity as satisfied for the time being, storing away what we are acquainted with as our sufficiently assured possession. New questions arise by superimposition of new systems of relevances of one kind or another.

2. It is not possible to give an account of the newly emergent motivational relevances without analyzing the ontological condition of man in the world, by which he defines the circumstances of his situation in accordance with his autobiographical determination. Our analysis will therefore be restricted to those elements of the biographically determined situation which themselves belong to the subjectively unquestioned world of things taken for granted. But since one set of these elements, originating in the biological requirements of our organism, consists in the need to come to terms with the subjectively defined environment (to dominate the circumstances by changing them, to perform actions gearing into the outer world), our motivational relevances will at least partially be determined by these elements.

Pragmatism, in a misplaced monistic attempt to build up a philosophy from one single aspect of human life, has given a curious monopoly to the motivational relevances originating in the organismic necessity to come to terms with the environment. Others, such as Scheler, have discovered a pragmatistic motive even in our perception and in the general character of our knowledge.[22] The radical pragmatist tries to reduce any kind of knowledge to its usefulness for coming to terms with the surrounding world, and the success or failure to do so even becomes a criterion of the truth of such knowledge. By definition, then, on this view our idea becomes topically irrelevant if it is not motivated by relevances related to the supreme purpose of coming to terms with the surrounding world. In other words, the radical pragmatist takes the system of in-order-to relevances, the sum total of which is the plan of life by and for the sake of which we come to terms with the environment, simply for granted—it is for him a kind of unadmitted a priori. To be sure, we are always interested in certain topics, and for the sake of determining these we have to interpret them adequately.

Yet such a position would be valid only if the level of reality constituted by our working acts gearing into the outer world were the *only* level of reality in which we live. Admittedly, this is the paramount reality (the home base for all the other levels of reality, which can be interpreted, then, as deviations from it). It is the paramount reality because only within it are sociality and intrahuman communication at all possible.[23] But there are many other systems of motivational relevances originating on other levels of our "attention to life" upon which we may and do bestow the accent of reality—among them, the levels of theoretical contemplation on which man tries to come to terms with basic experiences, and one in particular that reaches beyond all environmental factors originating in the circumstances of his situation within paramount reality: his basic experience,

22. The reference here is particularly to Max Scheler's *Die Wissensformen und die Gesellschaft, Probleme einer Soziologie des Wissens* (Leipzig, 1926). Schutz devoted three remarkably lucid essays to Scheler's thought: see *CP 1*, "Scheler's Theory of Intersubjectivity and the General Thesis of the Alter Ego," 150–79; and *CP 3*, "Max Scheler's Philosophy," 133–44, and "Max Scheler's Epistemology and Ethics," 145–78.

23. This sentence was marked for deletion.

namely, of the transcendence of his life, which transcendence itself makes the immanence of his existence at all possible. The system of motivational relevances originating on levels of reality other than that of paramount reality are simply discarded by radical pragmatism, and therewith are discarded the various systems of topical and interpretational relevances guided by such motivational ones. *Pragmatism is, therefore, not a philosophy dealing with the totality of human existence, but a description of our living on the level of the unquestioned paramount reality.* It is a typification and idealization of our being in a world taken for granted in every respect other than our concern with the "business of living."

But even this restricted purpose is only partially achieved by radical pragmatism. It offers a solution merely from the point of view of an imaginary, disembodied observer who is himself placed outside of any environment with which he must come to terms. *Pragmatistic theory of knowledge can never explain what the pragmatistic philosopher does,* just as behaviorism can never explain the behavior of the behaviorist.[24] Subjectively viewed (namely, from the experiences of the acting subject himself in his effort to come to terms with his environment), the system of motivated relevances by which he is guided is not only experienced as a system of interrelated in-order-to motives, but also as a system of interrelated genuine because motives. The latter withstand all rationalizations and are known as passions, hopes, fears, expressions of the metaphysically basic experience of our having been born into an already existing world in which we grow older and eventually die—that is, in a world which will continue to exist after our death as it existed before our birth.[25]

This objection to radical pragmatistic philosophy is not to be

24. For a more extensive critique of behaviorism and related stances, see *CP 1*, "Concept and Theory Formation in the Social Sciences," 48–66; and R. Zaner, "A Critique of 'Tensions in Psychology Between the Methods of Behaviorism and Phenomenology'", *Psychological Review*, *74* (1967), 318–24.

25. Schutz characterizes these as experiences of transcendence; cf. *CP 1*, "Symbol, Reality and Society," esp. 329 f., 337 ff., 353 ff.

construed as a denial of the importance of motivational relevances originating within the paramount reality of our working acts and which break down the seemingly self-explanatory knowledge taken for granted into an unproblematic field over against which problematical topics stand out. This is indeed a principal reason for bringing into question affairs which have hitherto been unquestioned—an action which induces us to undo the process of sedimentation of apparently sufficiently established knowledge. But it is not the only set of motivational relevances. Such motives for new questions, or for making questionable what was hitherto unquestioned, may originate on any level of reality.

3. Thus far we have dealt with newly emergent questions which originate in superimposed systems of motivational relevances. But new questions may, as we said before, also originate in superimposed interpretational relevances. Apparently, those interpretational relevances will refer, when they become questionable, to the "same" topics which in prior processes of sedimentation led to a sufficiently established acquaintance with them—that is, the character of familiarity is bestowed on them. Yet, as we also saw, this is a very loose way of speaking. *If new interpretational relevances supervene they can never refer strictly to the same familiar topic. Rather, they refer necessarily to the unfamiliar, atypical aspects of something typically known thus far*—which aspects were hidden up until now in the unexplored horizonal material. Again, there is a tendency in philosophy to refer all newly emergent questions to supervening systems of interpretational relevances, bestowing on the latter a kind of monopoly in the process of breaking down the field of the unquestioned and the undoing of the established sedimentations.

The philosophical doctrine promulgating such a monopoly is known as *operationalism*. The world is supposed to be pregiven as a matter of act, as a sum total of data each of which carries along from the outset its topical relevances, frequently assumed to be grouped under a pregiven hierarchical order. It is also assumed that there is a constant set of motivational relevances inciting the mind to transform an unclarified situation of questionable knowledge into a state of *warranted assertibility*. This transformation occurs by means of a set of operations which are nothing other than a system of interpretational relevances, a set of rules according to which horizonal material might be related to the topical kernel in order to determine its implications until the state of warranted assertibility has been reached.

As with any philosophical theory subsequently pursued by eminent thinkers, operationalism contains a certain amount of truth. Perhaps more clearly than other thinkers, operationalists have seen that all problems emerge on the ground of an unquestioned body of knowledge which becomes questionable in the course of the process of sedimentation. They have also seen that in undoing the sedimented habitualities we intend to reach a state of knowledge established sufficiently for the purpose at hand. This state has been reached if its assertibility is warranted, and that means, in the language used in this study thus far, that if by means of our inquiry the horizonal interpretational relevances have been made explicit up to a point which clarifies the topic at hand sufficiently, there are no motivational relevances left unfulfilled which would prompt us to carry the inquiry further. The problem at hand has then been solved, the warranted knowledge can be stored away until something novel emerges within our experiential field that is incompatible with and irreducible to our stock of warranted knowledge. If this occurs then another unclarified situation originates and further inquiry is then required. The interplay of operations starts again, or in our language new interpretational relevances supervene and the whole process of inquiry recommences.

Operationalism sees all this clearly, and has as certainly grasped the fact that the system of interpretational relevances is itself an element of our knowledge at hand and that it depends upon the topics, the facts, to which they refer. Precisely this defines the operational rules to be applied. In the realm of rational scientific knowledge these rules may be made explicit; and the totality of them constitutes the methodology of this particular science. In the realm of practice, these rules are the approved and tested procedures of handling situations, things, and men. Even logic can be conceived as a system of inquiry according to rules with the purpose of transforming unclarified situations into those of warranted assertibility.[26]

However, in every case operationalism has in view merely the system of interpretational relevances as the originator of inquiry. Motivational relevances are simply taken for granted, and the topical kind are either interpreted as emergent novelties or as the results of the operation of interpretational relevances. Now while it is true that methods refer merely to the ascertaining of what is interpretationally relevant, this latter concept refers to a topic at hand. How these topical relevances emerge is beyond the reach of operational rules and methodology—except, as we stated before, that interpretational relevances may make visible new aspects of the previous topical aspects hidden in the hitherto unquestioned horizonal implications (in which case, subthematization and even covering the prior topic may occur).

It is a fundamental error of the neo-Kantian school to believe that the method "creates"—whatever this term may mean—the object of inquiry.[27] Methodology—and its corollary on the practical level, namely recipes and maxims of action, ways of conduct, etc.—refers merely to the proper determination of what is interpretationally relevant with respect to a previously prevailing topic;[28] especially does it refer to the (scientifically and practically) correct use of typification, the ascertainment of the depth-level of inquiry, the delimitation of the purpose at

26. Schutz discusses these rules in detail in *PSW*, Ch. 5; and *CP 1*, "Common-Sense and Scientific Interpretation of Human Action," esp. 34–47. He has made numerous concrete uses of them in those studies collected in Part II of *CP 2*, esp. "Equality and the Meaning Structure of the Social World," 226–73.

27. Merleau-Ponty, despite many profound similarities to Schutz's work, has also argued this. Cf. *Phénoménologie de la perception*, pp. 90, 140, 261–62, 275 ff., passim (E. T., pp. 72, 120, 226 f., 238 ff., passim).

28. Schutz marked this sentence unsatisfactory up to this point.

hand, etc. Methodology can never establish what topic is relevant to us, nor can rules of operation supply the focus of our motivational interest. Important as the superimposition of interpretational relevances is for the restoring of the inquiry into problems stored away as no longer questionable, neither the interpretational relevances, as operationalism believes, nor the motivational relevances, as pragmatism believes, have a monopoly on or even a paramount function in these occurrences.

4. This becomes particularly clear if we consider that the necessity to undo the process of sedimentation of habitually possessed knowledge occurs at any time when supervening topical, interpretational, or motivational relevances clash with those taken for granted thus far. They may turn out to be inconsistent, incoherent, incompatible with the former to an extent which precludes continuing the idealization "and so on and so forth" and hampers the ongoing course of habitual expectations, especially protentions originating in the unquestioned use of the system of relevances thus far taken for granted. The extent of such inconsistency cannot generally be determined. As our static analysis of the structure of our stock of knowledge will show,[29] we carry along at any time a certain number of elements of our knowledge not consistent in themselves and not compatible with one another. This is so, on the one hand, because we live simultaneously on different levels of reality, and on the other, because by our autobiographical situation we are involved with different layers of our personality (even in that sector of the world on which we bestow, for the time being, an accent of reality). We assume roles, and especially social roles. Yet, as long as we are not compelled to face such a situation of conflict (that is, as long as no motivational relevances originate in it, leading us to make topical what has been hitherto beyond question) we disregard these inconsistencies and incompatibilities. *They are irrelevant, immaterial for our purpose at hand.*

As will be shown at a later point, it is an existential corollary to the ontological condition of man in the world that the totality of this world in all its diversity remains to him *fundamentally*

29. In Ch. 6.

incomprehensible, that his own finitude bars him from grasping the infinity of the universe.[30] In the paramount reality of the world of working—the foundation of all sociality—this phenomenon has its counterpart in the basic assumption of the social distribution of knowledge and the attempt to overcome this parceling out of knowledge by communication.[31] Regions of the unknown always remain, some of them possibly knowable, some beyond our possible knowledge. Of the former type, only a small sector seems to be worth knowing in terms of our actual autobiographical circumstances. These are the white spots on our maps of the universe, the unexplored regions, the exploration of which seems to be desirable or even necessary. We shall call these regions the *vacancies* (*Leerstellen*) of our knowledge, a term already used before (but whose full meaning for the structurization of our stock of knowledge at hand will have to be explained in the following chapter).

The undoing of our habitual possession of knowledge, the restarting of sedimentation, the retransforming of knowledge beyond question into questionable problems, the recurrent reinterpretations of what we know—all these lead to the fact that *once-filled vacancies may become vacant again,* that former vacancies are filled tentatively, that hypothetical "relevances provided that . . ." are developed with their own particular open horizons and their pertinent systems of interpretational and motivational relevances, that the modifications of the various conflicting systems of relevances overlap, requiring therefore their expansion or restriction, and that phenomena of covering, dropping, interruption, and the like occur.

It is impossible and also unnecessary to describe (by way of casuistics) all these possible interrelations. We have only to understand that the transformation of the unknown into knowledge, the dissolution of the known into new vacancies and vice

30. Schutz was able only to outline this analysis in the present study; cf. below, Ch. 7.
31. Schutz has studied in detail the complexities of language as used in communication in daily life: cf. *PSW,* esp. Ch. 3; and *CP 1,* "Symbol, Reality and Society," esp. 319–29 and 345–56.

versa, the entering into the hitherto unexplored horizons of hitherto irrelevant but possible knowledge, the creating of new systems of interpretational and motivational relevances—in short, that all these phenomenal transformations, creations, annihilations, the whole interplay of fulfilled expectations and frustrated anticipations (not to say the questionability of the sufficiency of our knowledge and the determination and redetermination of the purpose at hand) occur with a particular individual rhythm having their own transitional movements (flying stretches and resting places), their own unique articulations and even impulses of "quanta" (remembering our caution, expressed earlier, regarding this metaphor). *It is this rhythmical articulation of our mental life which is constitutive for our historico-autobiographical existence as human beings within this world.* Our own history is nothing else than the articulated history of our discoveries and their undoing in our autobiographically determined situation.

Chapter 6/The Stock of Knowledge at Hand
Structurally Interpreted

In previous chapters we have considered various features of what we called the process of sedimentation of our experiences by which our stock of knowledge at hand becomes constituted. The study of the genesis of this stock has shown that it is composed of manifold elements. Our experiences show different degrees of clarity and various stages of plausibility, from unquestioned acceptance in the form of blind belief, through the various forms of *periodeusis,* to the completed *diexodos,* or empirical certainty. Some of our experiences are simply grasped monothetically, while others can be referred to the polythetic steps in which they were built up; in view of this, our experiences have different degrees of distinctness. They are grouped into various more or less complicated meaning-contexts, dependent on the underlying network of retentions and protentions, recollections and anticipations, the functional unity of our organism, the apparent coherence of the objects of the outer world, the fringes of the symbolic system to which they pertain, the unity of the project of our action, and so on. Our experiences originate at different moments of our inner time, and by this very chronological sequence they show a particular profile as regards their structurization and coherence. Some are temporarily held in abeyance; others are the outcome of repeated processes of sedimentations and dissolutions—thus showing an immanent historical development. All these phenomena have been studied in their genetic development in the last section.

134 ALFRED SCHUTZ

It is now important to analyze, in *static* terms, the structure of our stock of knowledge at hand, describing in more general terms the various dimensions of it at any given moment of the individual consciousness. Except for some anticipatory allusions, we are still dealing with the fiction that this problem can be studied for a supposedly isolated mind without any reference to sociality. We are of course aware that this procedure involves the unrealistic assumption that our knowledge of the world is our private affair and that, consequently, the world we are living in is our private world. We deliberately disregard the fact that only a very small part of our experiences or knowledge genuinely originates within the individual himself; we recognize but here ignore the fact that the bulk of our knowledge is socially derived. In the same manner, we disregard the social distribution of knowledge and the particular phenomenon of socially approved knowledge. Yet, unrealistic as these assumptions are and however serious are the limitations thereby imposed on our study, they are justified by the attempt to work out certain aspects of knowledge exclusively relating to the individual mind. And keeping in mind this abstractive character of our presentation, our procedure is the more harmless in view of the third part of the present study, which has as its main subject the very problems deliberately disregarded here.[1]

A. The Dimensions of the Lifeworld[2]

At any moment of my existence I find myself in possession of knowledge of a certain sector of the universe which in the natural attitude I call, briefly, "my world." This world consists

1. Although this analysis is not included in the present study, the bulk of Schutz's work was devoted to these issues; precisely for this reason, he was constantly aware of the "abstractive" character of the present study.

2. Schutz began using this Husserlian term at about the time he wrote the present study. Cf. Husserl, *Die Krisis der europäischen Wissenschaften und die transzendentale Phänomenologie: Eine Einleitung in die phänomenologishe Philosophie,* edited by Walter Biemel, *Husserliana,* Band VI (The Hague, Martinus Nijhoff, 1954). See also Schutz's

of my actual and previous experiences of known things and their interrelations—known to me, to be sure, to different extents and in manifold degrees of clarity, distinctness, consistency, and coherence—and certain more or less empty anticipations of things not experienced thus far, and therefore not known but nevertheless *accessible* to my possible experience (and, thus, potentially knowable by me). My world (the world in which I have been thus far living and in which, through the idealization "and so forth and so on" so essential to my natural attitude, I expect to continue to live in the future) has from the outset the sense of being typically a world capable of expansion; it is a necessarily open world. In other words, my world has the sense of being from the outset merely a sector of a higher unit, which I call the universe—the latter being the open "outer" horizon of my lifeworld. *The possibility of transcending the lifeworld belongs to the ontological situation of human existence.*[3] What we subjectively experience determines our knowledge of being continuously "in situation," the circumstances of which are autobiographically defined. Human existence as well manifests itself in the emergence of novel experiences not related to the sum total of my actual and anticipated knowledge of my lifeworld.

1. The lifeworld is "open" in many dimensions. *Spatially*, it is open as regards all the objects of the outer universe, those within and those beyond my actual and potential reach in the broadest sense (which includes things and occurrences which can be brought within my immediate reach, my sensory field, with the help of devices already discovered or still to be discovered).[4] In the dimension of *time*, my lifeworld is open both past and future, in respect of my experiencing this world as having existed before my birth and as going to continue after

previously unpublished paper, *CP 3*, "Some Structures of the Lifeworld," 116–32. As noted in our introduction, this latter essay seems to have been taken from the present study.

3. Cf. *CP 1*, "Symbol, Reality and Society," 329 ff.

4. For Schutz's conception of "actual and potential reach" cf. ibid., pp. 306 ff. and 329 ff.

my death. Insofar as my lifeworld reveals *levels of reality,* or finite provinces of meaning, it is also open: the world of working, of imagination, of dream, and all the other intermediate realms connected with the many degrees of tension of my consciousness, those actually experienced as well as those potentially available for me. Finally, it is open in the dimension of *society,* in the sense that it includes as essential components of its meaning for my experience the lifeworlds of my contemporary fellowmen (and those of their fellowmen), the worlds of my predecessors and successors (and the worlds of my fellowman's predecessors and successors), and everything created by them and possibly to be brought about by their actions, and so on.

But despite the fact that the lifeworld is always open in these dimensions, *it is experienced by each of us as the world with which he is or may become sufficiently familiar in order to carry out the business of living.* It is the natural and social surroundings into which each of us is born, and the existence of which he simply takes for granted. Indeterminate as this world may at least partially seem to be, it is a world of *determinable indeterminacy.* It is the frame within which possibilities are open to us, the locus of realization of all of our open possibilities, *the sum total of all circumstances to be selected and defined by our autobiographical situation.* Our belief in its existence is the unquestioned foundation for all possible questions, the unproblematic ground for the emergence of all possible problems, the prerequisite for transforming any unclarified situation into warranted ascertainability.

2. Our knowledge (in the sense of our habitual possession of a stock of experience, acquaintance, and knowledge) of this world, however, has various degrees which refer to the structurization of the lifeworld into several provinces. This is not the place in our study to enter into all the details of this structurization;[5] we restrict ourselves here to giving just one example to clarify the interrelationship between this structuriza-

5. For these details, cf. "Symbol, Reality and Society" and *PSW*, esp. Ch. 4.

tion and the organization of our stock of knowledge at hand.

We mentioned before that within our lifeworld the world of working stands out as the paramount reality, which corresponds to the highest tension of our consciousness (the state of wide-awakeness characterized by our highest attention to life). This is the sector of the lifeworld into which we may gear with our actions, which we can modify, manipulate, and change. Yet this world of working is itself structurized in a particular way: a segment of it is *actually within our reach,* while other segments are merely *potentially within our reach*—whether they were formerly within reach and can be brought into our reach again (i.e. the world with *restorable* reach), or whether they never have been within our reach but with respect to which we have the plausible expectation that they can be brought within our reach under certain conditions (world within *attainable reach*).

Let us consider only the central sector of the working world: the world within our actual reach, from which the other sectors within restorable and attainable reach can be derived. At any moment of our existence, we take it unquestionably for granted that a part of our lifeworld *can be manipulated,* changed, and dominated by our action. But this is possible only if these actions are indeed performable within the actual circumstances prevailing within this sector—that is, within the order of things in space and time and their mutual interrelationships. This *performability* presupposes that according to our stock of knowledge at hand, there is a certain set of things or events, called *means accessible to us,* which, if appropriately handled and put into play, will bring about a certain state of affairs aimed at in our projects of actions, called *ends.*

Now, it might require the full interplay of topical, interpretational, and motivational relevances to ascertain the ends to be aimed at, to find the possible courses of action necessary to bring about this state of affairs, to select from among all possible courses of action those which are performable because the means are accessible to us, and finally from among those performable actions those most appropriate under the prevailing circumstances. If such is the case, nothing is taken for granted except the existence of the lifeworld, in which is included a province of paramount reality which again has a center that is within our actual reach. But in terms of this unquestioned foundation of open possibilities, the problematic possibility of choosing among projects of action is revealed, with all their adherent topical, interpretational, and motivational relevances. For instance, our previous experiences of the appropriate typical use of typical means for bringing about typical ends might itself become a topical relevance, requiring us to enter into the inner horizon of such relationships in order to make explicit the hidden implications of the means-ends mechanism involved. If such a situation occurs, a topical problem has been created which has to be solved before being stored away; and how this is done is the particular dilemma faced by having to choose among projects of action that will be described in detail in the second part of the present study.[6]

Yet the choice among projects of action does not always become topically relevant, nor is it always necessary to gain a clear and distinct insight into the mechanism by means of which the state of affairs aimed at is brought about. There is a level embedded in our world of working within actual reach, within which not only is the state of affairs to be brought about taken for granted as a self-explanatory end, but also where the appropriateness and accessibility of specific means to bring about this state of affairs is simply accepted as a matter of course beyond question. This is the level of our *routine actions* in daily life, of the manifold chores customarily performed in a rather automatic way according to recipes which were learned and have been practiced with success thus far. We take it for granted without question that the recipes having thus far "stood the test" will also prove to be efficient in the future, insofar as typical ends will have to be brought about by typical means. We are so conversant with these typical situations and their typical interrelationships, and our expectations that things will go on

6. Not included in the present study, but see *CP 1,* "Choosing Among Projects of Action," 67–96.

as they have thus far seem to us so plausible and self-explanatory ("so obvious"), that we follow our routine, as we call it, as a matter of course so long as nothing interferes which might hamper the normal (that is, the unquestioned and hitherto efficient) process of our ongoing activities.

3. This level of the working world within our actual reach, within which there is at any given time a plausible chance to apply tested recipes of action, is called my *world of routine activities*. Within its limits everything is—always until counterproof—familiar to me and, therefore, taken for granted. It is a world of familiar topics, familiar interpretations, and even the system of motives governing my actions are just habitual possessions of previous experiences and thus far fulfilled expectations. Not only do my genuine because motives remain unquestioned (and even invisible); this remains the case in any sector of the lifeworld so long as we are living within our activities (in the broadest sense, including awareness, perception, and attentional apperceptions) and so long as nothing makes us "stop and think" and grasp in a reflexive attitude the set of our because motives.

But within the world of routine, even our in-order-to motives are simply taken for granted as a matter of course, since they are founded upon the unclarified and opaque because motive which says in effect that our purposes are attainable, our actions performable, our habitual possessions of experience well tested. *Once taken for granted, the system of motivational relevances determines a system of topical relevances* which, paradoxically expressed, are topical merely as a matter of course— that is, topical not as a theme, as a problem to be solved, as something to be questioned anew, but as "topics *in* hand," as formerly thematic questions which have been "definitely" and exhaustively answered, problems "once and for all" solved and stored away. So to speak, these topics-in-hand have lost their interpretational relevances. It at least appears that all horizontal material had been brought into the thematic field when the topic was still outside the sphere of mere routine; by becoming routine, by bringing it "in hand," the open inner and outer horizons have seemingly disappeared. Or, expressed more adequately: they were just cut off, and therewith were cut off all possibilities of reinterpreting the topic-in-hand. Yet, all this holds good only until further notice: if something hampers the ongoing routine action, the topic-in-hand prevailing up to then may go "out of hand," the topic may become again a theme and all its horizons again open to interpretational questioning.

From the point of view of the organization of consciousness, the topics-in-hand within the world of routine are no longer within the thematic kernel at all. They remain, to the contrary, in the margin. I may think over my vital practical or theoretical problems while walking, eating, shaving, smoking a cigarette, and so on. The consummate player of a musical instrument will, while playing at sight, perform the routine operations necessary to produce the required sounds; topically directed to the meaning of the particular piece of music reproduced, he will automatically translate the signs of the score into sound (unless a particular technical difficulty obliges him to make the correct fingering topical, or to examine an unusual notation as to its correctness).

Our analysis of the world of routine as a substructure of the world within our actual reach—which in turn is just a sector of the world of working and refers to our lifeworld as a whole, the lifeworld with its openness in various dimensions to the universe—had first of all the aim of giving an example of the interrelationship between the immanent structurization of the lifeworld and the organization of our stock of knowledge at hand. It will also serve us in what follows as a starting point for determining the precise meaning of "the world beyond question." Full insight into the structurization of the lifeworld will be obtained only in the fourth part of this study, in which we will investigate the structure of multiple realities.[7] In order to ascertain the meaning of the world beyond question, we will now proceed with the investigation of the organization of the stock of knowledge at hand.

7. Not included in the present study, but see *CP 1,* "On Multiple Realities," 207–59.

A word of caution is in order here, however, in order to avoid a possible misunderstanding. In our preceding example we dealt with routine work as a particular form of the world within my actual reach, which itself is the central layer of my world of working. This example should not be construed to mean that there is no routine activity possible in provinces of our lifeworld other than that of working, that is, that no routine would exist with respect to activities not requiring bodily movements gearing into the outer world. *The routine is a category which can be found on any level or activity and not only in the world of working,* although it plays a particularly crucial role within this paramount reality—if for no other reason than the fact that this world of working is the locus of all possible social intercourse and that working acts are a prerequisite for all kinds of communication. The study of the various forms of action in Part II of this essay[8] will give us the opportunity to discuss the various forms of routine on various levels of human conduct. Here, investigating first of all the structure of the stock of knowledge at hand and its interrelationships with the various provinces of the lifeworld on the one hand, and on the other with the systems of relevance, we are satisfied that *routine activity on every level is characterized by the particular transformation of the topical, interpretational, and motivational relevance structures already delineated.*

B. Knowledge of Acquaintance and the Concept of Familiarity

In his *Principles of Psychology,*[9] William James distinguishes two different kinds of knowledge, which he calls "knowledge of acquaintance" or "knowledge of," and "knowledge about." There are many things and relations about which we have a more or less vague and unclarified knowledge, but relatively few with which we are acquainted, as it were, through and through. We could expand this by subdividing the realm of things, events, and relations about which we have knowledge

8. Not included in the present study.
9. James, *Principles of Psychology, 1,* 221 f.

into those states of affairs *of which we are merely aware,* those *of which we are conscious,* and those *of which we are informed.*

But *is it not possible to interpret all types of knowledge as different degrees of familiarity?* We have already noted that the term "familiarity" always carries the sense of "familiarity sufficient for the purpose at hand." To familiarize oneself sufficiently with things, events, relations means, therefore, to acquire an amount of knowledge adequate to carry out or to further our purpose at hand. This purpose may be a theoretical or a practical one, and if we give the term "pragmatic" a meaning broad enough to cover both then, so it seems, we can agree with Scheler that our knowledge is always codetermined by a pragmatic motive. In these terms, then, the error of radical pragmatism would be to interpret the activities of consciousness, in the narrow sense, as actions in the outer world having exclusively practical aims, in particular aims designed to satisfy biological needs.

We have already pointed out that as soon as the objects of our experience are thought to be known sufficiently for our purpose at hand, no further research or inquiry is deemed necessary. The problem involved in the previous topic has been solved, and the acquired knowledge can be stored away and preserved as a habitual possession of my stock of experiences —neutralized and dormant, to be sure, but ready to be reactivated and used at any time if typically similar problems are encountered. We have already investigated the particular relationships between familiarity and the systems of relevance, between familiarity and typification, and between the expectations involved in the typical familiar knowledge and the idealizations of "and so forth and so on" and "I can do it again." It thus seems that through this analysis we have also sufficiently explained the various categories of knowledge which James had in mind when he distinguished between knowledge of acquaintance and knowledge about.

Yet, such an interpretation of our results involves a dangerous oversimplification. There are other dimensions of our stock of knowledge involved which we have now to examine.

1. To begin with, not all the elements of the stock of knowledge are simply stored away for further use. Some are not "dormant" although it can be said that they are *neutralized* in a particular way. Some of these elements are *permanently present* and never released from grip, although they are not present within the kernel of the thematic field of consciousness, but always present in its margin. In a later section we will analyze many of them. [10]

A few examples should suffice to clarify the issues here. In the first place, there is our knowledge of our own body, not only of its position in space, the tension and relaxation of our muscles in repose and movement, but more importantly the limits of our body which alone defines and determines what does not belong to our bodily self—therewith as well what is and is not within my reach. Another permanent possession always present in the margin is our knowledge that the outer world exists; the objects in it exist and exercise influence upon us by offering resistance, by requiring our effort if we want to change and manipulate them by our actions. This knowledge of wordly objects, moreover, includes the knowledge that we are not alone in the world, that there are fellowmen, social institutions, society, and so on. All this is known to us, not in the way of mere familiarity, but as a permanent content, if not prerequisite, of our conscious life. *This knowledge is not "at" hand; it is "in" hand,* because no state of mind could be imagined in which these experiences were not present—although only in the margin, as integral elements.

Of other elements of our knowledge it can also be said that they are *in* rather than *at* hand, although in quite another sense. Such elements as these are not an integral part of every imaginable state of mind or experience; they are not necessarily omnipresent in the margin, but the business of living does not, nevertheless, permit us to let them entirely out of our grip. We think here of the routine activities analyzed in the preceding section. These show a curiously paradoxical relevance structure: they have an outstanding but permanent relevance. However, as

10. See below, Ch. 7.

long as they are unhampered in fulfilling their specific functions, they are not conceived as being within the thematic field; they are no longer experienced, in other words, as topics in themselves, and we may venture to say that they have lost their topical relevance. Precisely insofar as, and when, they become transformed from elements of knowledge *at* hand into those *in* hand, they have become artificially isolated from their inner and outer horizons. Having the highest degree of familiarity, they do not need further interpretation or definition of their functional character. Having their fixed (i.e. "routine") place in the habitually possessed chain of means-ends relations and —important enough—functioning as specific means for well-circumscribed *specific* ends, they are more than typified: they are *standardized* and *automatized*. Their motivational relevances proper are buried under layers of superimposed relevance systems, in relation to which they function just as specific means to bring about specific ends of a higher order. Thus, these elements of our knowledge *in* hand are characterized by the fact that their proper system of topical, interpretational, and motivational relevances has been truncated. *Routine knowledge*—which term we shall use for this subdivision of our knowledge in hand, to differentiate it from the subdivision of *existential knowledge* already mentioned[11]—is knowledge for the sake of other knowledge, the relevance system of higher order pertaining to the latter supplying the lost, truncated relevance systems properly belonging to the former. Thus, the elements of routine knowledge are no longer experienced as topics in thmselves; they seem to be objects pertaining to the lifeworld as such, within which they have their well-defined place and function. By their habitual use for specific ends, they have acquired the character of instruments, utensils, tools. We shall therefore speak of *the implementary character of routine knowledge-in-hand.*[12]

11. Schutz refers to that kind of knowledge he discussed in the preceding paragraph: knowledge of my own body as mine, of the world and its objects, of my fellowmen, society, and the like.
12. Routine knowledge seems to be roughly parallel (at least) to what Heidegger calls "circumspection" (*Umsicht*). Both routine and

It will be helpful to give an illustration in which the transformation of knowledge *at* hand into implementary routine knowledge *in* hand is clearly discernible. Any student of a foreign language can determine the moment when the foreign idiom ceases to be a habitual possession at hand and can be freely mastered as a tool for conveying his ideas. This is precisely the moment when the so-called passive reading knowledge of the foreign vernacular turns into active speaking knowledge; the foreign terms are then not merely recognized when encountered, but as it were they offer their services when needed, they are ready for active use, they are utensils *in* hand. Existential and routine knowledge are elements of our stock of knowledge at hand which cannot be explained in terms of mere familiarity.

2. The term "familiarity" itself covers many heterogeneous situations, and James' distinction between "knowledge of" and "knowledge about" seems to aim at the separation of at least two of them. We are familiar with things, events, and the relations prevailing among them; we know of certain causes producing certain effects, of certain means for bringing about certain ends. But frequently we are familiar (in the sense of "knowledge of acquaintance") with merely the "That" of these affairs, and have at best a "knowledge about" their "How" and "Why," or we simply ignore the latter entirely. A few examples from daily life will suffice to illustrate these two dimensions of familiarity and knowledge.

Every cook knows that an egg boiled in hot water for three or four minutes will become "soft boiled," and that if the cooking process is continued, it will become what we call "hard boiled." Yet the highly complicated events taking place in the

---

existential knowledge, on the other hand, seem roughly equivalent to what Heidegger designates as *Zuhandenheit*. See *Sein und Zeit,* pp. 101–12 (E. T., pp. 134–48). It might be suggested, however, that not only does Schutz delineate what is *"on* hand" (Heidegger's *Vorhandenheit*) and what is *"at* hand" (*Zuhandenheit*), but that his analysis shows the necessity for a further sphere—viz. what is *"in* hand" (which is of several kinds).

chemical structure of the albumin which produce this state of affairs is not known at all by the cook and perhaps even not entirely clarified by chemical science.

Again, I know that the cherry tree in my garden will blossom in spring, thereafter be covered with leaves, and then bear fruit; finally, that it will lose its leaves later on and be bare in winter. I know all this as a matter of course, and if I am prone to religious or poetic feelings, this metamorphosis will evoke in me admiration and awe of the recurrent miracle. But not being a biologist, I do not know what really happens within the organism of itself to bring about this cyclical change; and the explanations which biologists have given me thus far seemed to me rather scanty and beside the point.[13]

We live in our present culture surrounded by a world of machines and dominated by institutions, social and technical, of which we have sufficient knowledge to bring about desired effects, without, however, much understanding (if any) of how these effects have been brought about. We turn switches, press buttons, operate dials, and know as a matter of course that the bulb of the lamp over my desk will give some light, that the elevator will go up to the desired floor, or that I have a good chance to hear over the telephone the voice of the party I want to talk to. Not being an electrotechnician or physicist, I have no knowledge of what happens when I manipulate any of these devices and, indeed, I am not at all interested in this. I am, however, very much interested in the state of affairs to be realized by manipulating the appropriate devices through which (this I know in the sense of being fully acquainted with the phenomenon) I have an excellent chance to attain the de-

13. As Camus remarks when explanations are pushed we always end up in poetry. Cf. *The Myth of Sisyphus, And Other Essays* (New York, Vintage Books, 1955): "Yet all the knowledge on earth will give me nothing to assure me that this world is mine. You describe it to me and you teach me to classify it. You enumerate its laws and in my thirst for knowledge I admit that they are true. You take apart its mechanism and my hope increases . . . All this is good . . . But you tell me of an invisible planetary system in which electrons gravitate around a nucleus. You explain this world to me with an image. I realize then that you have been reduced to poetry: I shall never know." (p. 15).

sired end. Yet I remain rather ignorant concerning how these effects are brought about. I just know that "somehow" my turning the dial of the telephone sets in motion several mechanisms of one kind or another (I have a vague knowledge of the existence of an underground telephone network, of exchanges, perhaps of electric impulses in general), and that by all these unknown or only vaguely known events I will be able to talk to my distant friend.

If I put my letter into a mailbox, I am perfectly familiar with the fact that there is a very good chance that after a certain lapse of time my message will reach the address. Of course, I know also the existence of post offices, and that the mail is carried by railroad, airplanes, or vessels from one place to another. But I am not acquainted, nay I am even not eager to become acquainted, with how this whole organization works.

I receive money for my work and can purchase merchandise and services with this money, but unless I am an economist I have no precise knowledge what money really is, whether and how prices are a function of the currency, and so on. And, listening to discussions or reading the papers of very learned economists, I am not even sure whether they have knowledge of acquaintance with or just knowledge about the phenomena involved here.

Finally, talking to a friend, I take for granted that he will understand my thought if I use the appropriate terms of our common vernacular, but I do not know how it comes about that the fact that my larynx produces certain sound waves reaching my friend's tympanum has the miraculous power to convey my thought to him.

It could be said that the difference between the two levels of knowledge can still be explained by its sufficiency for our purpose at hand, which is determined by the systems of motivational relevances prevailing at the time in any particular situation. In mailing a letter, my motive is to convey the message contained in it to the addressee, and it is in the main immaterial whether I expedite this letter by way of the regular mail services or by dispatching a messenger to deliver it. The result of either procedure is to get the letter in the hands of the addressee in an appropriate time, and it is only this result which is motivationally relevant to me—not to mention the case in which my motive might be merely the conveying of the message contained in the letter, which could be achieved as well by using the telephone, calling the person, and so on.

The limits of our prevailing motivational relevance have been expressed by such words as "we are not interested in" the details of the mechanism. By this very lack of interest these details can never become topically relevant and therefore cannot originate a system of interpretational relevances set in motion to solve the problem involved in the topic. In the present case we may assume that the knowledge of the details involved would be as a matter of principle attainable by me, if I thought it worthwhile to bother with the procuring of the necessary information (say, by studying a manual on mail service, visiting a post office, talking to experts, and so on). But in this case there is no inducement for me to do so. For my present purpose at hand in this action such information is not required; it is sufficient for me to know (and this in terms of full acquaintance with the matter) that the institution of the mail service exists and that in the regular course of affairs this institution will render these and those services to anyone who behaves in a particular standardized way (e.g. by writing the correct address on the envelope, affixing the due amount of stamps, depositing the letter at a specific place, and the like).

This explanation is doubtless correct, but it rather hides than reveals a more important problem. It shows that our curiosity is satisfied and our inquiry stops if knowledge sufficient for our purpose at hand has been obtained. But this breaking up of our questioning is founded on an existential element of all human knowledge, namely the conviction of the *essential opacity of our lifeworld*. We cannot penetrate with the light of our knowledge into all dimensions of it; we may succeed in making some of them semitransparent, and only fractions of the latter translucent. Paradoxically expressed, we are familiar (in the sense of knowledge of acquaintance) with the fact that large dimensions of our lifeworld are unknown to us. This is nothing else but another expression for the experience of transcendency which is immanent to our lives.

But what do we mean precisely by stating that certain dimensions of our lifeworld are unknown to us? The term is more than equivocal.

a. Something may be unknown to me because I have never tried to explore it. If I did I might attain knowledge; I might have the chance to make this particular layer of opaqueness transparent. Such would be the case in our last example. But it would be better to use the term "unquestioned" rather than "unknown" in this case. The unquestioned dimensions of our lifeworld are merely unknown because I have disregarded their investigation. I did not care to do so because there was no incentive, no motivational relevance to make this region the topic of my investigation. In the language of daily life, I consider the unquestioned but questionable regions of the lifeworld as in principle knowable but not worth knowing—at least "for the time being," "in the present context," or "from our point of view." As long as this region does not interfere with the matters I am topically concerned with now, I take it simply for granted as a matter of indifference. Yet I feel free to start its exploration at any time, to make what is hitherto unquestioned topical; and on the other hand, I am aware that at any time events may occur which impose upon me to start such an inquiry. I may then have to explicate hitherto unexplicated features of my lifeworld.

The unquestioned region of my lifeworld is, therefore, merely "unknown until further notice." This is another expression for the circumstance that what we call our stock of knowledge at hand is not a closed realm. Our actual knowledge refers to potential knowledge in the same manner in which we found that the sector of the world within my actual reach refers to a region within my potential reach. We may therefore speak of *the unquestioned world as the realm of attainable knowledge*— and just this is the first meaning of "unknown."

b. We have seen that the world potentially within my reach

contains also a sector which was formerly within my actual reach and which can again be brought potentially within my actual reach. We called this sector the world within restorable reach. In the same way, my potential knowledge refers to elements which were once actually known but are no longer actually known, although this knowledge might be restorable. This realm of restorable knowledge is the second meaning of the "unknown world."

Two cases have to be distinguished within this particular category of the unknown—that which was formerly known and knowledge of which can be restored:

i. The formerly actual knowledge has been lost and has to be reconstructed. This loss may either refer to some elements of a unified meaning-context which has been preserved in my actual knowledge; or the meaning-context itself may be lost, whereas some of the elements which constituted it have been preserved. The first case may occur if knowledge acquired polythetically is actually accessible in a monothetic glance, whereas the polythetic steps leading to this sedimentation are forgotten.[14] The second case may occur if one of the unifying factors from which the meaning-context originated disappears. This would be the case, for instance, if for pathological reasons the functional unity of our organism breaks asunder; or if the apparent coherence of an object of the outer world proves to be inconsistent; or if the fringes of a symbolic system lose their connective power; and so on. What has to be restored in the first case, by renewed inquiry, is the lost inner horizon of the preserved meaning-context; in the second, the lost outer horizon of the preserved elements has to be restored for reestablishing the forgotten meaning-context.

ii. It is possible, however, that the formerly actual knowledge has not been entirely lost, but is merely covered by supervening knowledge without having been completely an-

14. For example, having once learned the proof of the Pythagorean Theorem, I now know it is true (monothetically) but can no longer recall all the steps of the proof (polythetically).

nihilated. Rather, it has just been transformed, modified, neutralized, but it can be restored again under particular circumstances. This kind of restorable knowledge, which is merely hidden by actual knowledge, requires our special attention; Section 3 below will be devoted to this analysis.

c. The realms of attainable and restorable knowledge represent two provinces of the unknown which are potentially knowable. The third meaning of "unknown" which we must now discuss is of an entirely different character. Suppose we are eminently interested in solving a topically relevant problem. The system of interpretational relevances comes into play; by means of its reference to our actual stock of knowledge at hand we succeed in determining certain aspects of the problem at hand. But there are other aspects which resist any interpretation, which cannot be brought into any relation with our stock of knowledge at hand. In other words, some elements inherent in the topic at hand are unknown to us and never have been known.[15] These are precisely the atypical, the unfamiliar, aspects of the problem with respect to which, however, it is of the highest motivational relevance to familiarize ourselves. Our interest to know the unknown is the decisive difference between the present case and that of attainable knowledge discussed under (a). In the latter case, the unknown was merely unquestioned but believed to be knowable. It remained unquestioned because it was for the time being of no concern to us. In the present case, however, we may well be vitally interested in acquiring knowledge of the unknown aspects of the topic at hand, of becoming fully acquainted with it. But the object remains at least partially opaque, and there is thus no reason to believe that the knowledge looked for will be attainable and that the problem involved can be satisfactorily solved at all. Yet we have to be more precise: we know, under our assumption, many things *about* this topic, but we cannot arrive at a full knowledge of acquaintance with all its aspects. Our knowledge of the object is spotty, there are gaps, enclaves of the unknown in the

15. Schutz marked this sentence unsatisfactory.

midst of the known (or as we shall call it, *"vacancies"* [*Leer-stellen*] in our knowledge). Are we entirely unable to form plausible expectations concerning how these vacancies can be filled? Is the unknown, in the sense of vacancy, forever hidden to us? Here a new problem emerges: namely, the problem of the aporetic function of the vacancies of our knowledge, which will have to be discussed in a separate place.[16]

To sum up: *the structurization of our stock of knowledge at hand*—disregarding the manifold events leading to its sedimentation—*cannot be explained in terms of familiarity sufficient for the purpose at hand alone.* The reason for this fact is the essential opacity of our lifeworld, which withstands the acquisition of complete knowledge of acquaintance. There will always be, by necessity, regions of the unknown. But the term "unknown" may refer to the unquestioned, knowledge of which is in principle attainable; to lost or covered knowledge, which is in principle restorable; or to genuine vacancies or enclaves in our knowledge, from which the problem of aporetics arises.

3. We have thus far used such terms as "world taken for granted" or "world beyond question," "familiarity" and "sufficient knowledge," without giving desirable precision to their meanings. We spoke also of neutralization and actualization, refraining from investigating what has to be understood by both. Is our knowledge of the world a mere awareness or is it a positing[17] of the world involved? Is our belief in it a mere acquiescence or is it a well-founded belief, a conviction that the world is as it is known by us? Are our habitual possessions just sedimentations of former activities, of "customs" in the sense used by Hume, or are there endorsements in the validity of our knowledge (in Husserl's term, *Stellungnehmende Akte*)[18] of whatever kind involved? And if so, how can these acts of endorsement be explained?

16. See below, Sec. (4).
17. That is, a "positing" in the epistemic sense ("to posit"). As Husserl expresses it, the fundamental characteristic of consciousness' experiences of its objects is doxic (i.e. a believing, with different modalities, ranging from positive belief to positive disbelief). Cf. *Ideen 1*, Secs. 103–06, 120.
18. Cf. *Ideen 1*, Sec. 103.

But what does knowledge of the negative, or familiarity with what the lifeworld is not, mean in terms of the organization of our stock of knowledge at hand? How is a doubtful situation possible? How is it possible that our expectations and anticipations may explode?

We believe that the answer can be found in the realm of the unknown (which we have described as a subcategory of restorable knowledge), namely in the situation in which the formerly actual knowledge was not entirely lost but survives—although neutralized, modified, and covered by supervening knowledge. *All forms of negation (including doubt) refer to previously actual knowledge* (in whatever form of plausibility) *by which what is actually negated was believed to be acceptable or was merely taken for granted.* In terms of this formerly actual knowledge, there originated an expectation which has not been fulfilled by supervening experiences but has rather *exploded,* but without having been entirely annihilated. It survives as formerly actual and now "covered" knowledge; but it is knowledge which has been *stricken out* or *bracketed.* However, all doubting or negating refers to a former state of knowledge relating to typically the same object in which that which is now denied or doubted was believed to be positively valid or at least taken for granted. The opposite of what is ascertained by supervening knowledge was at least anticipated as something sufficiently plausible, at least as a *pithanon.*[20]

In other words, the formerly actual and now covered knowledge is motivationally relevant for the negative statement which itself thereby becomes an element of the original system of interpretational relevances related to the restorable topic. Any negation or situation of doubt can emerge only within such a structure of relevances. The judgment, "The whale is not a

20. The following passage was struck out by Schutz: "The insight, 'No fish breathes by lungs,' presupposes a previous assumption that there are fishes or that fishes may probably be found who do so—perhaps the whale whom I mistakenly considered to be a fish. I anticipated something which was at this time unknown: possibly, probably, plausibly, desirably, unfortunately as fish will be found who breathes through lungs. I have to have dissected a [the sentence was not completed]."

fish," refers to a previous state of my—or, to anticipate the impact of intersubjectivity, of someone's—belief that the whale is possibly, probably, plausibly, desirably, unfortunately, a fish. It has the shape of a fish, it lives in the water, and so on. I have to have learned or found out that the whale breathes through lungs and not through gills, that it is warm-blooded, reproduces like mammals and nourishes its young with milk, and so on, in order to cancel my previous belief that the whale is a fish and thus to make the statement, "The whale is not a fish." This statement is, however, meaningful only in relation to the former, opposite belief. From the point of view of formal logic, the statement, "The whale is not a mineral," is equivalent to the statement, "The whale is not a fish"—and both are true in terms of both Aristotelian and symbolic logic. But the first is motivated by its relevance to a former belief, the latter is not.

To vary our example, we could note that the insight, "All fish breathe through gills," leads to the equivalent one that "No fish breathe through lungs"; and having ascertained that the whale breathes through lungs, I may come to the conclusion that the whale is not a fish. But I may also arrive at the conclusion that the whale is an "atypical" fish insofar as it does not breathe through gills, and this might lead me to the belief that there are some fish which do not breathe through gills— and that therefore the proposition, "No fish breathes through lungs," is false. This belief, taken in isolation, is not so implausible as it seems if I compare it with the fact that there are mammals which are oviparous (such as the platypus) and are therefore in this respect "atypical" mammals. Yet, in either case we must refer to a "criterion" of typicality which is nothing else than the interpretational relevance structure inherent in a given topic which seems to be unquestioned and simply taken for granted. What is typical, what is atypical in the world as taken for granted, what has to be taken as the rule and what as the exception, can be explained *only by the underlying structures of relevance*.

It is first of all the system of interpretational relevances inherent in a topic to be known sufficiently for the purpose at hand which has to stand the test of consistent coherence in the course of supervening experiences, and which permits one to discontinue the investigation and thus to "store away" this piece of knowledge as now being *in* hand and not subject to further questioning. If, however, by a supervening experience this system of hitherto consistent interpretational relevances breaks asunder, then the "inactual," "bracketed" but "restorable" knowledge may give rise to new motivational relevances and motivate us to revise the plausibility of the belief taken for granted thus far. However, *it is always the meaning-context of the knowledge taken for granted which (1) constitutes the framework of all possible future questions which might be interpretationally relevant to the topic in hand, and which (2) becomes motivationally relevant for looking at the situation hitherto taken for granted as an unclarified and questionable one which has to be restored and revised.* Thus, the unquestioned knowledge stored away is the locus of all possible future statements relevant to the once-constituted topic which might enter into a meaningful context with it. In terms of our example of "The whale is no mineral," neither of the two prerequisites seems to be given. Nevertheless, this statement makes sense, but not from the point of view of the topic of determining what the whale is. It is another topic which permits this statement to be interpretationally relevant. In the present case it is the topic of the scientific investigation of the meaning-structure of negative propositions with which we have concerned ourselves in the present section.

In more general terms, *negation and all forms of modalization* which we find in our actual stock of knowledge at hand *refer to now potential and formerly actual knowledge which has been covered and is hidden by elements pertaining to the actual knowledge at hand.* The important fact is that the formerly actual knowledge survives in a neutralized form, as (definitely or temporarily) stricken out, as discarded in my actual knowledge at hand. *In this sense,* but only in this sense of being covered and neutralized, *it is one of the forms of the unknown.*

Yet I may revert to it, reactivate it; precisely this I do in the situation of doubt. "Am I right in negating now what I formerly believed to be true? Is not the now negated assumption perhaps preferable? Let us reexamine the whole situation!" How such a process of resuming discarded sedimentations of knowledge starts has been described in a previous chapter. Here it is important only to understand negation and modalization as particular forms in which formerly actual knowledge survives as potential and thus as retorable knowledge.

There are other forms of such a relationship which should be at least briefly enumerated. There are the various forms of the pathology of knowledge, studied by Cassirer in the third volume of *Philosophy of Symbolic Forms,*[21] and in particular the language disturbances referring to formerly actual and in principle restorable knowledge. What Goldstein calls the loss of the "abstract attitude"[22] can be explained in these terms. The actual knowledge of the patient permits him to think only in what Goldstein calls the "concrete" attitude. Formerly, the abstract terms were within his reach, belonged to his actual stock of knowledge at hand. Now they are buried because the pathological state has broken asunder the meaning-context unity created by the organism. The theory of repression in psychoanalysis would be another example. Finally, it must be determined whether the relationship between Gestalt and ground should not be referred to problems of negation.[23]

21. Cf. Cassirer, *Philosophy of Symbolic Forms, 3,* 205–77.
22. Cf. above, Ch. 4, n. 26. As Schutz points out (*CP 1,* "Language, Language Disturbances and the Texture of Consciousness," 262), "In the concrete attitude we are given over passively and bound to the immediate experience of unique objects or situations. Our thinking and acting are determined by the immediate claims made by the particular aspect of the object or situation to which we have to react as it is imposed on us. But the abstract attitude—also called the categorial or conceptual attitude—involves choosing a point of view from which we ascertain the situation, taking initiative, making a choice, keeping in mind simultaneously various aspects of a situation, grasping the essential, thinking the merely possible, thinking symbolically, and, in general, detaching the Ego from the outer world."
23. This concluded the original manuscript, dated "Estes Park, August 16, 1951." Among Schutz's papers, however, were found two

4. The theory of vacancy.[24] We do not know which *occupation* Carneades' man has, *where* the scene takes place (New York? Athens? The same man in a New York apartment or in Korea?). Alternatively *snake* or *pile of rope?*

When are the given elements "sufficient" for interpretation? To what extent do the *given* (well known, taken for granted as beyond question) moments predelineate the "vacancies" which remain undefined? Is there a kind of aporetic of typicalities which can be fitted into these vacancies? How is the contour of *missing* pieces which "fit" (as perhaps in a "puzzle") predelineated through the Gestalt of the vacancy (even where the choice is limited to the still unused pieces remaining—which, however, are *ready* for use)? It there are, however, no suitable elements in the "stock" of unused pieces—are they lost, were they ever there, must they first be "made"?

From here on a phenomenological analysis of the structural model is perhaps possible of that which is expected, anticipated, [as] graspable in protentions (intuitively?)—indeed even a new interpretation of πιθανός as categories of modalization. In general, seen from this perspective, the concept of modalization achieves a new sense; even *negation* presupposes an expected

---

further sections of this study. One, which comes first here, is only a brief sketch of a theory of "vacancy"; it was written in German and accompanied with an outline of the theory written in English (the former was dated April 3, 1951). The second piece is a longer and connected discourse on the "Biographical Situation" and was intended as the concluding chapter of this part; it is Chapter 7 of the present study.

Both pieces are included here, in the order indicated, precisely as they were written (but the German has been translated). The pages dealing with vacany have a title page, with the title, "Philosophie der Leerstelle (Vacancy)," and a motto, *Hic egregie progressus sum.*

24. There are a number of serious problems with translating this section. Being only a sketch, many sentences are incomplete, the punctuation does not always conform to the sentence construction, verb tenses do not always agree with their subjects, and so on. Moreover, the section as a whole is not consecutively developed with consistency. I have tried only to correct the obvious grammatical and syntactical errors in the text, retaining as far as possible its original sketchiness, in keeping with the editorial decision to refrain from tampering with Schutz's original text.

anticipation. "No fish breathes through lungs" presupposes the assumption that all or some fish do this—perhaps the negation of the motivational relevance in the case of the whale—which negation *constitutes* the "vacancy" in the sense of "puzzle." "Possibly," "probably," "plausibly," "hopefully," "unfortunately," the whale *fits* into the "vacancy." On the other hand: I must first of all dissect a whale in order to know that it breathes through lungs and therefore is not a fish. Perchance his gills are only "hidden," "covered."

Also, the problem of "covering," which so occupied Husserl, belongs here.

Moreover: (1) All of the foregoing is too static. In the constitutional analysis the construction of the stock of experience which is "at hand" (stock of knowledge at hand although not *in* hand) is disclosed as a succession of the filling-in of vacancies of what is still not known, but these vacancies are already *typically* predelineated through the contour-lines of what is already known (?). This is possibly a *definition* of the meaning-context, in any case of the underlying structural context. Also, the "unknown" can be grasped as the "no longer known," as "destroyed vacancy"—a hand has thrown the already completed puzzle pieces into confusion, the indicated contours are no longer contours; or, they are covered. Similarly, references to disturbances of the "abstract" attitude in Goldstein's work.[25] In the "concrete" [attitude], I can fill in only the "sharp," the "well-circumscribed" vacancies; the more "abstract" the objects are, i.e. the fewer "clues" yielded by the elements remaining to be "filled in," then so much the more can typically different elements (typically indeterminate elements) be fitted in —the more empty, anonymous, the more usable, but the less "suitable," the less "relevant." This [is] also a clarification of Gestalt, of the "background," probably as well of the "constancy-hypothesis."[26] [The] *principal question:* all that can be exhibited in the prepredicative sphere; can modalization, even perhaps the axioms of formal logic of contradiction—the principle of contradiction—excluded middle [*Dritten*] and so on—

25. See above, n. 22.
26. See above, Ch. 4, n. 37.

be reduced to this prepredicative structure? And how is it in the logic of daily life? Is not the concept of vacancy and contour connected with the structurization into theme and field (horizon)? Is not the shifting ray of attentional advertence *directed* through the contours? And all these are immanent time-processes. The distinction between polythetic and monothetic advertence (which is becoming more and more important) proves itself here as a component of the "quantum theory of consciousness." What I succeed in apprehending, in the polythetic construction, as *contour or fragment of a contour,* allows me to find the element which is *missing, suitable.* If I succeed in this, then I can look monothetically at the material formed according to the "picture" (successfully fitted together on the "table"). The tabula rasa idea corresponds to the *table;* association psychology works with preformed puzzle elements. Thus, both have seen an important problem but at the same time missed the point. For everything depicted here in spatial and therefore inadequate metaphors is the fixed product, the result, of processes of the stream of consciousness, of what Bergson call *durée.*

But perhaps there are quite tiny puzzle elements. Leibniz' *petites perceptions* do not form contours (in this metaphorical sense), therefore they are perceived but not apperceived (similarly, Maine de Biran). Gurwitsch's "awareness" here has its limit.[27] The amorphous structures of undetermined but determinable inner horizons, "passive synthesis," could be interpreted as the evolvement of contour. Neutrality and positionality is the way from the perceived to the apperceived explicatum (if one can legitimately speak of an "explicatum" at all at the level of the prepredicative).

2. All this is clear as regards the vacancies whose contours are predelineated, pertaining to what is anticipated but still not known within my own consciousness. Knowledge, however, is socially distributed. We work puzzles *together.* What already indicates a picture for you (although an incomplete one affected with vacancies), delineates *for me* the choice of elements which

27. Cf. Gurwitsch, *The Field of Consciousness,* pp. 237–45, concerning the awareness of the "inner horizon."

possibly fit together. This is the true reason why, *before* all communication, there must already be a certain conformity of the relevance-isohypses of the partners. Nevertheless the same vacancies have differing aspects for you and for me, for I am "hic" and you "illic," our autobiographically determined situational elements are necessarily different, and so on. These [are] the riddles of the subjective and objective sense. Also, the solution of the problems pertaining to "socially [derived] and approved knowledge."

"Social Role"—the decision to want to consider only elements of a certain typical contour as appropriate. (This is a "convention" in the sense of the decision in chess that a rook *may* be moved only in a straight line. To that extent, the definition covers everything normative. However, the "convention" in this sense has its own history, its social motives: it is itself [a] contour vacancy to be filled.)

Perhaps operationalism and pragmatism enter here.[28]

3. (Probable outline for chapter titled "Philosophie der Leerstelle [Vacancy])."

The interconnectedness of the three forms of relevance

The concept of stock of knowledge at hand (system of interpretative relevances)

    a. Genetically as sedimentations of previously constituted relevance structures

    b. Statically: The isohypses; knowledge of and knowledge about; the world taken for granted; the blind belief; and so forth and so on

    c. Organization of the stock of knowledge at hand; the pragmatic motive; the familiar and the novel; the unknown; theory of the unknown

    Ambiguity of the term "unknown":

    A. What has never been known and has to be known

    B. What was formerly known and has been lost

    C. The "hidden" ("covert" = *verdeckte*) knowledge

---

28. This concludes the passage written in German; there follows the outline, in English, of the theory of vacancy.

A. The typic of expectation as an aporetic problem.

    a. The "blank": vacancy and missing link (preliminary)

    b. Typicality of the missing link preconstituted by surrounding topical and interpretative "data" that is *accepted* (taken for granted) habitual possessions

B. The "lost" knowledge:

    a. The elements are lost: Theory of the inner horizon

    b. The context is lost: Theory of the outer horizon

C. The "VERDECKUNG":

    a. The origin of negation as referred to previous contrary expectation

    b. The modalizations; possible; conceivable; imaginable; credible; likely; practicable; feasible; workable; achievable; accessible; obtainable; hoped for; dreaded; unfortunately

The abstract and concrete attitude of Goldstein. Loss of abstract attitude. Pathology of knowledge: Cassirer III; Psychoanalytic problems; Negation and Gestalt—form and ground [?]

Systematic Theory of the Vacancy

A. Static Interpretation

I. The impossibility of full knowledge:

    a. *"Undurchschaubarkeit" der Welt* ["opacity" of the world]

    b. Selective activity of the mind: "attraction" and attentional ray (Husserl): but this meandering of the attentional ray is motivated (as to be shown later (a) by "steering" through the contour lines (b) autobiographically within the meaning of motivational relevances)

II. Typification

    1. Origin of typicality in the prepredicative sphere *(Erfahrung und Urteil)*

    2. Typicality and anonymity: sharply outlined or well-determined "puzzle elements"; "rounded off" or anonymous parts are interchangeable and replaceable

    3. Typification in the predicative sphere: S is—in addition to $Q, R, \ldots X$—*also P;* The P-ness of $S;$

III. Typification and Vacancy
    1. Vacancy from the outset typically predetermined, namely by typicality of surrounding contour lines: theory of the inner horizon as locus of typically compatible elements
    2. Vacancy—in the sense of missing link—determines also outer horizon namely in the sense of "meaningful context"
    [Marginal note: Perhaps these are two kinds of vacancy!]
    3. Vacancy as the aporetic locus of: (α) all possible topical relevance structures; (β) all possible interpretative relevance structures
IV. The spheres of incompatibility (Husserl's *Unverträglichkeits Sphären*)
    The sum of the angles in a triangle is the color red
    Whitehead's problem
    The "predicative argument"
    The "liar" and the paradoxes

B. Genetic Interpretation

I. The activities of the mind in constituting vacancies and contour lines
    a. the passive synthesis: sameness, similarity, likeness, *Überschiebung* [overlaying], *Überschneidung* [overlapping]; "accouplement" and representation;
    b. awareness and reflective attitude
    c. the attentional ray as steered by the contours
    d. expectations and anticipations: The situation of doubt; How is "explosion" possible? The dilemma and the alternative
    e. limits for filling-in missing links:
        (α) The essentially actual experiences
        (β) Leibniz' *petites perceptions:*
        (γ) Maine de Biran and the *inconscient*
        (δ) Freud and the unconscious
        (ϵ) Bergson's theory of remembering and forgetting
II. Positionality and Neutrality
    a. the habitual acquisition as the sedimentation of pre-

vious acts of filling in vacancies

b. positionality as belief in the world as taken for granted. Is the world as taken for granted still topically relevant and if so to what extent?

c. first meaning of neutrality:

The world as taken for granted is the realm of determinable indeterminacy (Husserl) or the unclarified situation to be transformed into warranted ascertainability (Dewey)

d. second meaning of neutrality:

The multiple realities and the reciprocity of perspectives

Particular problems of the paramount sphere of reality of daily life: the project—is it a modification of neutrality?

[the category of accessibility and performability. Details under the chapter, "Action," in the third part.]

III. The time structure of interpretation

a. monothetic and polythetic ray (Husserl)

b. resting points and flying points (James)

c. the quanta theory of consciousness

(a) What subdivisions of the meaning context are possible?

(b) Gestalt [the musical theme]

d. The phenomenon of recurrent reinterpretation; filled vacancies may become vacant again; the problem of history and historical existence (especially of autobiographical experience) as a quantum problem of consciousness

C. *Recapitulation of the Theory of Vacancies*

(a) Hume's concept of habit and belief

(b) The tabula rasa theory and the phenomenological psychology of the natural attitude

(c) Theme and field; again the problem of topical relevance.

(d) Bergson

"les deux ordres et le desordre."

D. The Interpretational Relevances
a. Establishment of missing links *in* the vacancy
b. Establishment of missing links with the meaning context.
c. Thinking of daily life and scientific method.

E. Transition to Motivational Relevances
Preliminary character of all these

Chapter 7/The Biographical Situation[1]

In the preceding chapters we gave, in a very rough and sketchy way, a survey of certain structurizations of our stock of knowledge at hand and the interrelationships among the various systems of relevance involved in the notion of familiarity. In discussing these matters we frequently had the opportunity to refer to the biographically determined situation of the self within the world—without, however, indicating precisely what this term means.

A. Structurization by Orientation: the "Frame of Reference" (Urarche Erde)

At any moment of my conscious life I find myself within the world, and my position in it—in time, space, nature and, as will be discussed only later on, as a man among fellowmen—as it appears to me is what I call my situation within the world. I am therefore, as French existentialists like to put it, always "in situation."[2] But this situation has its history, and certain of its elements are exclusively events within my own biography. Any situation refers to a previous one out of which the actual one developed. To the biographically determined elements of the situation belongs among many other things my stock of knowledge actually at hand, together with my convictions, opinions, beliefs of all degrees of plausibility referring to the world be-

1. This chapter was originally conceived as the concluding section of Part I (and was labeled Section X).
2. See above, Ch. 4, n. 36.

yond question. It includes as well my systems of topical, interpretational, and motivational relevances, my actual interests
and the systems of plans which select, out of the indeterminate
field of the world beyond question, those elements requiring
more exact determination and which are therefore problematical. Moreover, there belongs to the biographically determined
elements of my situation the particular structure and genesis of
my stock of knowledge at hand—which is, of course, in many
respects unique and singular. In part, this uniqueness consists
of what I know, with its figurations of relevance, shades of
clarity, distinctness, and purity, as well as what I believe to be
certain, probable, possible, plausible. It is possible, however,
that all these structural elements of my knowledge are shared
with others. But what is not shared with others is the particular
order in time in which this knowledge has been acquired by
me and the intensity with which it has been experienced—in
brief, the whole history of my conscious life. Insofar as my essentially actual experiences (which are not communicable) and
the events restricted to my inner life (imagination, phantasy,
dream, etc.) form part of this history, they are also included in
the biographically determined elements of the situation.

Furthermore, the system of my habitualities (including my
reactions, skills, abilities, gifts, as well as my ability to act, my
power) belong to the biographically determined elements of the
situation. To act shall mean here not only to gear into the outer
world and to change it by bodily movements, directly or indi-
rectly (by using tools), nor only the possibility of performing
kinesthesias, but also mental activities such as thinking through
a problem, living in a world of imagination, etc.

Here we have to anticipate a possible objection. It might be
admitted that these occurrences within my inner life have co-
constituted what I actually am: namely that I am and know
myself to be thus and so and not otherwise. It could be objected,
however, that it is a fallacy to include those elements in the
biographically determined situation inasmuch as this situation
is defined as referring to my position in the world, whereas for
example my dreams or phantasies do not refer to the world.

The answer to this objection is that everything depends upon the sense we give to the notion of "world." Our imaginary objector is obviously inclined to restrict this term to the natural world which *surrounds* the self, and in this sense some events of my inner life certainly have no reference to the surrounding world and my situation within it. Yet it seems to us that to restrict the term merely to the surrounding world—that is to Nature in the broadest sense (including not only the physical but also the social and cultural Universe)—would be a restriction hampering our future endeavors.

Anticipating a discussion which will follow later on, let us give one example: It is from our biographically determined situation that we draft, by acts of phantasy, a certain course of future conduct which may or may not be transformed into a project (with the possibility of being practically carried out within this world, and which therefore may not as such even refer to the *surrounding* world). We do not want to exclude applications of our insight into the structure of the biographically determined situation to occurrences of inner life of the aforementioned kind. World, therefore, is not only Nature (that is, the surrounding world), but any realm of intentional objects of our experience.

Notwithstanding this terminological clarification, we want to begin with an analysis of the situation of man within the surrounding world of Nature; and we shall even restrict our investigation in the present chapter to nature in the sense of the physical universe, whereas the discussion of our situation within society and culture shall be reserved to following chapters.[3]

I am, then, in the midst of the surrounding world, and at any time of my conscious life I find this world structured from the outset in specific ways. In order to understand this structurization we have to forget what we have learned from science about the structure of Nature; we must endeavor to give as true as possible a description of how Nature is naïvely experienced by

3. Not included in the present study, but see *CP 1,* "Symbol, Reality and Society," esp. 329–39 and 347–56; and *CP 2,* "The Dimensions of the Social World," 20–63, and "Making Music Together," 159–78.

any human being, without taking into account the various schemes of interpretation, idealization, and generalization developed by science and especially modern natural science. This may lead us to certain statements which might at first sight appear self-explanatory or as truisms. But since our purpose is the description of the structure of Nature as taken for granted, it is exactly that kernel of our experience of Nature which we believe to be self-explanatory and not worth putting in question which we seek to study. To give an illustration of what we mean: when describing the structure of Nature as it appears to man living naïvely in his surroundings, we have to forget the teaching of Copernicus and the subsequent developments in modern astronomy. The natural system of reference for man, the unmoved and unmovable ground upon which and with respect to which all possible movements are interpreted is the surface of the earth—the "primal arch" *(Urarche),* as Husserl called it.[4] In man's naïve experience it does not *seem* that the sun "rises" in the east and "sets" in the west, it *is* so. Let us imagine, says Husserl, how a child born on a vessel which sails along the coast would interpret his impressions of the gliding shoreline. To this "skipper's child," the deck of the vessel on which he was born and moves around is the only "unmoved" ground and frame of reference for interpreting all possible movement. To him, it is not the vessel which glides along the unmoving shoreline, it is the shoreline which moves in relation to the unmoved deck. The surface of our earth is to us, in this sense, the "primal arch" upon which we "skipper's children" are born and which alone we know as the unmoved ground in reference to which not only our locomotions and those of our fellowmen and animals occur, but in reference to which also the sun and the stars move around. If it is true, as Copernicus tells us, that the movement of the sun is merely an appearance, that the change of day and night is caused by the rotation of the earth around its axis, we, living naïvely in our surrounding nature, are not interested in this fact. It is not relevant to us

4. Cf. Husserl, *Ideen* 2, 52–54; *Cartesian Meditations,* pp. 44, 50, 53, 61.

(namely, not interpretationally relevant) so long as we are topically concerned with the world as taken for granted. Until Copernicus' theory, it was generally taken for granted that the sun rises over the mountain, is at midday in the zenith, and sets at evening in the sea; and this movement of the sun around the earth is still taken for granted by all those human beings who have never heard of the theory of Copernicus, by children, by primitive tribes, etc. It is taken for granted without question that there are seasons, that the vegetative life on the surface of this earth during these seasons undergoes a life cycle, etc. It is from this point of view—say, that of the tiller of the soil—immaterial (that is, topically, interpretationally, and motivationally irrelevant) whether the seasonal cycle is due to the revolution of the planet Earth around the sun or to the intervention of a god. What Copernicus did was to put in question what seemed to be hitherto beyond question. His system of topical relevances was quite different from that of the tiller of the soil, or of the man living naïvely within the surrounding nature. It was motivationally relevant to him, in his biographically determined situation, to dedicate himself to a particular topic: the study of the movements of the celestial bodies. The system of topical relevances thus constituted led him to the well-founded conviction that the system of interpretational relevances taken for granted without question since Ptolemy had to be put into question and be replaced by one more consistent with the topic, etc. In short, I have to be interested in the topic of astronomy in order to consider Copernicus' theory as relevant. But being interested in astronomy—or in any kind of science—I have put in question what seems to be unquestionably taken for granted by the man living naïvely within his surrounding world.

B. My Own Body: éspace vécu

Nevertheless, also for me, one who lives in a world taken for granted without question, this world has as well a specific structure which is also taken for granted. There is first of all one privileged object within this world which is present, if not appresented,[5] at every moment of my conscious life, namely my own body.[6] It is the "carrier" of my organs of perception—that is, it is affected by other objects and therefore is privileged. It is the "vehicle" of my kinesthetic and locomotive movements, the "instrument" by which I can gear into the outer world and change it by affecting other objects, and therefore again, it is privileged. Yet the way of speaking of my own body as a "carrier," "vehicle," and "instrument" is dangerous and careless. I *am* my body and sense perceptions, I *am* my hand grasping this or that object. My body is the form in which my self manifests itself in the outer world. All this has been analyzed in an excellent and careful way by Sartre and Merleau-Ponty, who continue the endeavors of Bergson, Husserl, Scheler, and Heidegger.[7] It is not our intention here to give a summary of their findings or to enter into an extensive phenomenological description of our experience of our own body. We only want to make a few remarks referring to the structurization of the world beyond question founded upon this crucial experience.

Our starting point has to be the fact that, for each of us, his own body and its habitual functioning is the first set of experiences taken for granted without question. We deliberately refer to its "habitual" functioning and not its "normal" one. If I am deaf or blind, certain dimensions of the world accessible to others are not accessible to me. I may learn from others *that*

5. Cf. above, Ch. 3, n. 13.

6. On the question of the "mineness" of the body, see above, Ch. 4, n. 34. In addition, see Husserl, *Cartesian Meditations,* Sec. 44; Husserl, *Ideen 2,* esp. 62–63, 68, 145–46 (and Schutz's critical review of this, *CP 3,* "Edmund Husserl's Ideas, Volume II," 15–39); Gabriel Marcel, *Metaphysical Journal* (Chicago, H. Regnery, 1952), and *Le Mystère de l'être,* esp. Vol. *1* (Paris, Aubier, 1951) (English trans., *Mystery of Being* [Chicago, H. Regnery, 1951]).

7. The seminal work of Gabriel Marcel should also be mentioned here. See above, n. 6; *Du Refus à l'invocation* (Paris, Gallimard, 1940) (*Creative Fidelity,* tr. by Robert Rosthal [New York, The Noonday Press, 1964]); *Être et avoir* (Paris, Aubier, 1935) (*Being and Having,* tr. by Katherine Farrar [New York, Harper Torchbooks, 1965; by arrangement with Dacre Press of A. & C. Black, Ltd., London, 1949]); and *Position et approches concrètes du mystère ontologique* (Paris, Vrin, 1949).

there are sounds or colors; yet in my deafness or blindness, sounds or colors are not elements of the world I take for granted without question. If I am paralyzed I may see and take for granted that other people move around freely, but the experience of locomotion (namely of my power of moving from place to place) does not belong to my world as taken for granted—although I may experience mobility if for instance my wheelchair can be moved about. As mentioned before, we have deliberately (although artificially) restricted ourselves in the present chapter to the analysis of the world taken for granted by a supposedly isolated individual, and we therefore have to refrain from any references to the existence of fellowmen and to their world beyond question. To be sure, the blind person knows that the world taken for granted by his fellowmen has features inaccessible to him, and he may even accept without question what he learns from them of their experiences of the world. But in his own experience of his world there are no colors, visual perspectives, etc., he could take for granted. For the sake of simplicity we will disregard in the following paragraphs the case of the handicapped person.

My body, says Merleau-Ponty, summarizing his analysis of its spatial dimension,[8] is not for me a fragment of space; on the contrary, space would not at all exist for me if I had no body. The space thus experienced through the intermediary of the body is, first of all, a space of orientation. My body is, so to speak, the center 0 of the system of coordinates in terms of which I organize the objects surrounding me into left and right, before and behind, above and below. Where I am—that is, the place of my body in outer space—is Here; everything else is There. Seen from Here, objects appear in certain specific distances and perspectives; they are arranged in a certain order, some presenting only one surface to me whereas their other sides are hidden; some objects are placed before or upon others, covering the latter totally or partially. This space of orientation has its dimensions: things have length, breadth,

8. Schutz refers to Merleau-Ponty's *Phénoménologie de la perception,* p. 119; see Part I, Ch. 3.

depth. All experiences of this space carry along open horizons of variability and constancy: of variability because, by a kinesthetic movement of my eyes, or by turning around, I may change all the perspectives and even the scheme of orientation (what was formerly left is now right, etc.); of constancy because, at least as a matter of principle, I may reestablish my previous position and reverse my kinesthetic movement in order to find the same objects in the same aspects and arrangement as before. Secondly, the space experienced through the intermediary of my body is space "lived through" (*éspace vécu*, as Merleau-Ponty calls it); that is, it is the open field of my possible locomotions. I may move within this space, transform my former There into a Here, seen from which what was formerly a Here turns out to be now a There. Through my movement, the center of the system of coordinates in terms of which I organize the objects in orientational space is shifted; distances, aspects, and perspectives change. What was previously distant and appeared relatively small is now of considerable size, whereas what was formerly near but is now distant seems to have lost in size. Formerly hidden or covered aspects of things or objects become visible and vice versa, as I move around. Nevertheless, the apparent change in size and the new vistas of these objects do not induce me to believe that what I am now perceiving are different objects: they are experienced as the same objects but appearing now as "seen from another point of view," "under a different angle." In the language used in previous chapters: my locomotion does not change the topical relevances connected with the objects perceived; they are the same objects but are now interpreted differently. Strictly speaking, we cannot say that the system of interpretational relevances has been *shifted* by my locomotions. I have only supplemented it by additional interpretational relevances which were implied in the original system and have now become explicit. The same holds for the system of topical relevances involved: in the change of aspects the same objects present in the course of my moving around the main topic are preserved, but what were then merely implied topical relevances have now become explicit.

C. The "hic" and the "illic"

All these are well-known and frequently studied phenomena; they are mentioned here simply because they are generally taken for granted and naïvely accepted as self-explanatory. Precisely because of this, however, they prove to be constitutive structurizations of the world taken for granted. It is, for instance, a trivial commonplace that I can not be at two places at the same time. This statement, however, taken for granted and true as it is, is by no means self-explanatory. Is it so beyond all possibility of doubt that I cannot occupy two different places at the same time, since I can obviously do two different things at the same time (for instance have a conversation while walking around, or think while writing)? What is really stated in this supposed truism is a fundamental ontological condition of our being in and experiencing space through the intermediary of our body. It refers to the fact that the location in space where my body actually is—and this place alone—acquires from this very fact the unique character of a Here over against which all other spatial locations are There and, more precisely, are There seen from my Here. The Here is unique because it may, after having become a former Here and actual There, be conceived as a "Wherefrom," "Whereto," "Wherein," "Whereon," etc. All these relations of orientation make sense only with respect to an actual There, never with respect to an actual Here— which, being the center of the whole system of orientation, always has the coordinate value of zero.

Yet it could be objected that the location of my body at the Here, its particular position in space, belongs to the biographically determined situation, and that orientational space and space-lived-through as taken for granted beyond question have to be explained independently of such subjectively determined circumstances. This objection, however, would miss the point for the following reason: of course, the particular Here at which I find myself at the present moment is biographically determined, and therewith the particular system of coordinates in terms of which I organize the surrounding objects in my orientational space is determined in the same way. Yet it is a structural element of the world beyond question that it is always organizable and organized relative to any Here of any subject within the world, and that its features are the same regardless of the location of this actual Here.

D. World within My Reach[9] and Topological Organization

This is only the starting point for further analyses. Through the experiencing of my body as Here, the world becomes organized into a sector *within my reach* and another *beyond my reach*. More precisely, we find the innermost kernel of the sector within my reach defined by the limits of my body itself. I am at any moment of my conscious life aware of these limits as I am aware of the position of my body in space, of cold and warm, etc.

The next layer of the world within my reach is what I can grasp with my limbs, especially with my hands—the so-called manipulatory sphere, which G. H. Mead considers to be constitutive for the notion of reality.[10] Next, there are things within my earshot or my field of vision which, although not within the manipulatory sphere, might be brought within it by locomotion or with the help of appropriate devices. It belongs probably to the naïve experience of the world taken for granted that it is assumed, until counterproof, that any object within the reach of my senses can also be brought, by appropriate locomotion or devices, within the manipulatory sphere.[11] Children want to grasp the moon or the stars and run for the golden cup on which the rainbow supposedly stands. It is not beyond question that there are visible or audible objects which nevertheless cannot be brought within any manipulatory sphere. But being visible or audible, these things are still, in a broader sense of this term, within my reach.[12]

9. See above, Ch. 6, Sec. A.
10. See G. H. Mead, *The Philosophy of the Present* (Chicago, Opencourt, 1932), pp. 124 ff.; and *The Philosophy of the Act* (Chicago, University of Chicago Press, 1938), pp. 103–06, 121 ff., 151 ff., passim.
11. Schutz marked this sentence unsatisfactory.
12. Schutz added the following note to this sentence: *"Unhegeblatt über* [lack of control over] movable and unmovable things. Concept of control."

As to the sector of things beyond my reach, it is necessary to distinguish between things which were formerly within but are now beyond my reach, because either the things have moved or my body has. My experiences of these objects carry along the expectation that they might be brought back into my reach if I assume my previous position or if I run after them. Another sector refers to things which neither are nor have ever been within my reach, but which I expect could be brought within it by bodily locomotion or appropriate devices. This case will become of special importance when we study at a later point the structurizations of the social world taken for granted without question.[13] We assume it as given until counterproof that any object of the outer world actually beyond my reach but within yours, my fellowman's, reach could also be brought within my reach if I changed places with you—that is, if I transformed my actual There, which is your actual Here, into my new Here.

The concept of things within or beyond my reach refers to my possibilities, my ability to move, and thus to the practicability of the projects of my future action. Yet the system of topical relevances to bring within my reach something which is for the time being beyond it is the starting point of a set of motivational relevances of the in-order-to type. They, again, are ontologically determined. Let us analyze a very trivial example: I am sitting at my desk in my study; the doorbell rings and I want to answer it. In order to bring the doorknob of the front door within my reach, I must stand up, go through my study, down the stairs, turn to the right, etc. I have to traverse a section of continuous space in order to reach the distant object. In my own home, in which the particularities and arrangements of the intermediate space are exceedingly familiar to me, it is situationally beyond question what I have to do in order to get from my desk in my study to the door at the front porch. This is a matter of course, of routine, because of habitually fixed, previous routine performances. In a similar situation in a house which is unfamiliar to me, I probably have to find my way by making topically relevant the simple phases leading to the de-

13. Not included in the present study.

sired result. Whenever and to whatever extent I have to make
the motivationally determined intermediate phases topically relevant depends, therefore, upon the biographically determined
elements of my actual situation. It belongs, however, to the
ontological structure of space taken for granted without question that, in order to get from point A to point D, I have to
traverse the intermediate points B and C. I cannot travel from
the American to the European continent without crossing the
Atlantic Ocean—either on its surface, or by airplane or sub-
marine. I cannot go from the East Side to the West Side of
Manhattan without crossing Fifth Avenue on the street level or
by subway. In building up my topical, motivational, and interpretational system of relevances, I have to take into account
the objective structure of space and situationally determine arrangements of things therein. I have to take these features into
account; they are important, they are relevant to me, but relevant in a particular way: they are *imposed* upon me, and thus
are not of my making; I have to take them without question as
they are. I may of course put in question whether I should make
my forthcoming trip to Europe by boat or plane, yet it is without question and I have to take it for granted that in one way or
the other I must overcome the obstacle of the Atlantic Ocean
interposed between New York, where I actually am, and London, where I want to go. To overcome the intermediate space
(if it is topically and/or motivationally relevant to me to reach
a distant point) is therefore relevant to me, and this relevance
is imposed upon me by the ontological structure of things. How
I may overcome the obstacle is, so to speak, within my discretion, within my power; it is relevant also, but this relevance is
of another kind. It is intrinsically relevant—intrinsic namely
with respect to the pre-established (imposed) topical and motivational relevances which are included in the everyday statement, "I want to go to London. Shall I go on the Queen Mary
or by the Pan American Airways?" Yet, to keep to our example, even these briefly sketched intrinsic relevances might turn
out to contain imposed elements. It might turn out that I could
reach London by taking a boat next Saturday at the earliest,

whereas it is topically and motivationally relevant for me to be there on Thursday. Then it is imposed upon me to take an airplane, and my freedom of discretion is thus restricted, say, to the question whether to travel by Pan American or another airline.

E. The Time-Structure

We have analyzed the spatial structure of the world taken for granted without question in some detail merely as an example and can now be briefer in discussing some—by no means all—of the other structural elements involved. The last variation of our illustration ("I have to be in London on Thursday") gives us the opportunity to study the time-structure of the world taken for granted beyond question.

Not only is the rhythm of outer time—the changes of day and night, the seasons, the vegetative life cycle, and that of the bodily time, breathing, heartbeat, etc.—taken for granted beyond question, but also the experience of inner time in its irreversibility and continuity. One of the most fundamental experiences is that of growing older,[14] the transition from infancy, adolescence, maturity through the declining years to old age. This time-experience is certainly connected with the physiological events within my body, but not restricted to them. Subjectively seen, it is an event in inner time. I was born, I grow older, and I have to die are three expressions for a single metaphysical fact determining the experience of our existence within this world. Yet this *metaphysicum*, which even the most inveterate behaviorist would hardly deny, is one of the elements accepted by any human being as an unquestioned and even unquestionable fact. Our growing older is of the utmost relevance to us; it dominates the highest interrelation of the system of our motivational relevances, our life plan. Experiencing our future as an undisclosed open horizon of the present (from which one single fact stands out in certainty, namely that we have to die,

14. See Schutz's marvelous essay, *CP 2*, "Making Music Together," 159–78; and *CP 1*, "Symbol, Reality and Society," esp. 316 ff.

not knowing when); our conviction of this certainty eventually translated into the feeling of our finity ("So little time," "It is later than you think"); these are perhaps the experiences of each human life which are of paramount relevance.[15] This relevance is imposed upon us in virtue of our human condition, as is the awareness of the irreversibility and irretrievability of time as such imposed upon us. And as to our beginning, our birth, the past which disappears in undisclosable darkness and of which we learn only from others, from our fellowmen—this is a taken for granted event which is the starting point for a set of imposed topical and motivational relevances. It is to each of us beyond question that the world—nature as well as society—existed before my birth; G. E. Moore has rightly shown the difficulty of qualifying the logical character of this statement: it certainly does not have an a priori character, but neither is it an empirical proposition, since it refers in every circumstance to a situation inaccessible to the experience of the individual who is convinced of its truth.[16] But it is taken for granted by every human being that he was born into a preexisting world and, more specifically, into a world of this and that particular structure, in this and that place, at this specific historical moment, into this and that social environment.

We are thus born into such an already existent world and into a specific situation, and this fact is one of the basic relevances imposed upon us determining our whole life in many respects. We have seen that any of our biographically determined situations refers to a previous one and that it can be interpreted as the sedimentation of all our preceding experiences. Our biography starts with our birth, and the situation into which we are born enters, therefore, as an integral element into all succeeding stages. It is at the origin of our system of topical, interpretational, and motivational relevances which now start to be built up. In a certain sense, we may say that the imposed

15. Compare Heidegger's notion of *Sein-zum-Tode, Sein und Zeit,* pp. 235–67 (E. T., pp. 279–311).
16. Cf. G. E. Moore, *Philosophical Studies* (Paterson, New Jersey, Littlefield, Adams & Co., 1959), "External and Internal Relations," pp. 276–309.

relevance of our human condition—that we are born into a world and a situation not of our making, that we inescapably grow older together, that within the essentially undetermined fact of our future one simple certainty stands out, namely that we have to die, uncertain when and how—we may say that these imposed relevances are at the foundation of the counterpointal structure of our consciousness of which we spoke in our introductory chapter.[17] All our interest in life, our building up of plans, our attempts to understand the world and our condition in it, in brief, the whole system of our topical, interpretational, and motivational relevances, can be conceived of as being intrinsic to these imposed relevances.

These fundamental imposed relevances are, however, by no means the only ones connected with the time structure of the world beyond question. It is characteristic for this structure that the dimension of inner time (of *durée,* the time in which the stream of consciousness of the individual unfolds) intersects with the biological time of our body, with the cosmic time of Nature, and—what will be discussed at length in the next chapter—with social time.[18] We live in all these time dimensions together but there is no one-to-one correspondence of simultaneity between the concurrent moments of events in each of them. The resulting gap imposes upon us a relevant *sui generis* phenomenon—namely, *waiting,* to be in readiness yet in suspense. Bergson was, so far as I know, the first philosopher to study the experience of waiting.[19] If I want to prepare a glass of sugar water (in his example), I have to wait until the sugar dissolves. The stream of my inner time goes on independently of the series of events in outer time for which I am waiting. Carrel and Lecomte de Noüy have studied a particular dimension of the biological time, the healing time of wounds—I have to wait to be cured![20] A woman with child has to wait, she has

17. Cf. above, Ch. 1, pp. 12–13.
18. Not included in the present study.
19. See Bergson, *Creative Evolution,* esp. pp. 12–13.
20. See Lecomte du Noüy, *Human Destiny* (New York, McKay, 1947, reprinted by The New American Library, Mentor Books); and Alexis Carrel, *Man the Unknown* (New York, Harpers, 1939, reprinted by MacFadden Books, New York, 1961).

to be prepared and ready until her time comes. The farmer, depending upon the cosmic time of nature, has to wait for the right time for harvesting. *Waiting is the expression for a system of relevances imposed upon us.* This system involves the problem of the "right time." There is a time for planting and a time for harvesting, and Ecclesiastes gives us a number of other examples for the "right time." Involved in this system of imposed relevances, however, is also the chronological order predesigned in the ontological structure of events beyond our control. The planting has to precede the harvesting; I have to depart from here before I can arrive there. This prearrangement of succession of the events in time frequently experienced in the form of the "post hoc," and frequently included in a blind belief in a "propter hoc," is first of all imposed upon us in the form of a chain of in-order-to motives. *In order to* go from New York to Chicago by train, I must go to Grand Central Station, purchase a ticket at the window, reach the appropriate track, board the right train—then I must wait until this train reaches my destination.

This dimension of time is analogous to that studied in the spatial dimension: If now, at the moment t_0, I am directed toward an event which will take place in accordance with the imposed chronological order only at the moment $t_0 + n$ or Δt_0, I must pass through all the moments between t_0 and $t_0 + n$ (or its increment Δt_0) and experience all the occurrences going on in my inner time between its corresponding moments. This of course is a very inadequate expression, which seems to suppose that inner time can be dissected into equal measurable moments, which certainly is not the case. But it is to be hoped that this brief analysis gives a rather graphic account of the difficult interrelationships of the various time dimensions.

Not only succession but also true simultaneity can be imposed. It is also ontologically prearranged what must, what can, and what cannot happen at the same time. Simultaneity may be interpreted as a limiting concept of succession and requires therefore no particular comment.[21]

21. The manuscript on relevance concludes here rather abruptly.